ON HOLY GROUND

The Impact of Psychotherapists' Spirituality on Their Practice

John P. Sullivan

University Press of America,® Inc.
Lanham • New York • Oxford

Copyright © 1998
University Press of America,® Inc.
4720 Boston Way
Lanham, Maryland 20706

12 Hid's Copse Rd.
Cummor Hill, Oxford OX2 9JJ

Library of Congress Cataloging-in-Publication Data

Sullivan, John P. (John Peter)
On holy ground : the impact of psychotherapists' spirituality on their
practice / John P. Sullivan.
p.   cm.
Based on the author's thesis (doctoral)—California School of
Professional Psychology.
Includes bibliographical references and index.
l. Psychotherapy—Religious aspects. 2. Psychotherapists—
Religious life. 3. Spiritual life. I. Title.
RC489.R46S84 1998   616.89'14—dc21   98-23788   CIP

ISBN 0-7618-1176-1 (cloth: alk. ppr.)
ISBN 0-7618-1177-X (pbk: alk. ppr.)

⊖™ The paper used in this publication meet the minimum
requirements of American National Standard for information
Sciences—Permanence of Paper for Printed Library Materials,
ANSI Z39.48—1984

Dedicated with love and gratitude to my parents

Yvonne Savage Sullivan

and Eugene Farrell Sullivan

who have planted and nurtured within me

the life of faith, learning, and service

Table of Contents

Foreword

For the past eight years I have had the great privilege - and education - of team teaching a week long seminar on "Psychotherapy and Spirituality" for Einstein Medical School's Cape Cod Institute. Each summer scores of mental health professionals, from psychiatrists to psychiatric social workers, clinical psychologists to psychiatric nurses, have gathered from around the country to reflect together on the problem and possibility of the integration of spirituality into clinical practice. One observation we have most frequently heard from these competent, self-reflective clinicians is that they experience a great relief in finally being able to "come out of the closet" as spiritually-committed individuals who are also trying to be responsible and skillful practitioners of the healing arts of psychotherapy. The language of "coming out," with its tacit association to sexual orientation, vividly testifies to the fact that sixty years after the death of Freud spirituality and religion still remains a highly problematic area within the culture of clinical training, supervision and practice. And yet, uniformly these women and men describe a deep personal and professional need to think critically, collaboratively and creatively about how their spiritual practices and perspectives relate to their psychological perspectives and together influence their clinical work.

Dr. Sullivan has written a book for the greater number of similarly motivated mental health professionals who may never make it to a Cape Cod Institute or similarly welcoming educational environment, but who have a passionate need to know that they are not alone in their concerns. More specifically, in his elegantly presented interviews, Dr. Sullivan offers what is still very difficult to find in professional conversation, let alone between two book covers: nuanced and richly described personal accounts of *how* five quite different but highly experienced and mature therapists think conceptually about the relationship of their spiritual lives to their therapeutic work, and *how* they actually work with that understanding in concrete clinical circumstances.

Dr. Sullivan's informants, though coming from quite diverse backgrounds and psychological and spiritual orientations, nevertheless bear an important family resemblance to the kind of professional that attends a Cape Cod Institute program. The five individuals who speak with such candor and eloquence in the following pages are persons who likely would not be comfortable describing themselves as "Christian psychologists," or "Buddhist psychologists" for that matter, even when their deepest commitments are fully grounded in those traditions. Like, I suspect, the greater number of their colleagues in the field, their own serious appropriation of spiritual traditions is non-ideological, pluralistic and open-ended. Their manifest concern for the freedom of conscience and radical particularity of the spiritual lives of their clients is a strong counterpoint to the legitimate concern that the therapist's religious or spiritual experience may translate into proselytizing or introduce confounding transferential factors into the therapy. What is striking to this reader about Dr. Sullivan's interviewees is that in many ways they anticipate and address some of the most important caveats and critiques of "spirituality" that come from classical psychological practice. By asking them the questions that educe this reflection Dr. Sullivan shows that he is not simply assembling an uncritical brief for the value of spirituality in therapeutic process.

Finally, each of these practitioners also demonstrates that the process of "integration" is a much more complex matter than simply finding ways of explicitly introducing spiritual themes or practices into the clinical context. Indeed, several demonstrate quite persuasively how the therapist's conviction of some kind of overarching meaning and significance, some sense of connection to a "More" has salient therapeutic impact whether or not it is consciously referred to in the work. It is a clinical adage, developing out a psychoanalytic object relations theory and family systems work, that the clinician should always be asking him/herself the question, "who all is in the room right now?" The burden of these interviews is to expand quite radically the referent of that "who all," and to demonstrate the potential difference that this makes.

In conclusion, Dr. Sullivan has written a book that will likely be most useful if the reader thinks of each of these five informants as colleagues and fellow seekers - not experts or gurus. Imagine yourself engaged in the kind of seriously playful and playfully serious conversations you would most want to have with such individuals - whether on a beach at Wellfleet or over a cup of coffee in your office. By passing over their own narrative you are encouraged and empowered to return to your own with fresh interest and understanding, to ask yourself the same questions that Sullivan posed, and to begin to answer them for yourself.

John McDargh, Ph.D.
Associate Professor
Religion & Psychology
Boston College
Department of Theology

Preface

This book had its beginnings in 1994 as I generated plans for my clinical dissertation for the Doctor of Psychology degree at California School of Professional Psychology in Alameda. It originated in my desire as a clinical psychologist-in-training to further cultivate my own commitment to a spiritually-based approach to healing and development, as well as hopefully to educate and inspire others who are also interested in a spiritually-integrated approach to their work as mental health professionals. What better way to grow in wisdom and understanding as one who attends to the minds and souls of others than to sit down with some "elders" in the field and to listen to their experiences of their spirituality and its impact on their clinical practice?

I am particularly grateful for the five "elder" psychotherapists who I interviewed and whose interview material is presented and discussed here in this book: Michael S. Hutton, Ph.D., Marianna Torrano, R.S.C.J., Ph.D., Alexander J. Shaia, Ph.D., Emma Bragdon, Ph.D., and Margery Cunningham, M.A., M.F.C.C. Each one has generously entrusted to me and to the readers something rich and sacred, not only about their work as clinicians, but also about who they are as human beings on a journey. I trust that their generosity will continue to yield abundantly.

I also want to express my deep gratitude to my dissertation committee members, Harriet Curtis-Boles, Ph.D. and Pamela A. Bjorklund, Ph.D. who were both consistently supportive, generous, and gracious in our working together on this study. The high quality of each one's assistance significantly contributed to making my experience of the dissertation reasonable and meaningful. The completion of the dissertation, my doctoral studies, and now this book has been generously supported and inspired by the love, confidence, wisdom, and prayers of my many devoted family members and friends. I am blessed by each of you. I am deeply grateful for you all. In particular, I would like to thank my brother Bill, Teresa Rapposelli, Psy.D., Ana Magalhaes, M.D., Susie

Fong, M.D., Joseph J. Driscoll, Laurie Stewart, Sally Clark, and Charles Terrell.

In addition, I am grateful for the support of my friends and colleagues at The Danielsen Institute at Boston University who share with me a vision of a spiritually-integrated approach to the practice of psychotherapy. I would also like to express my gratitude to James Finley, Ph.D. Finally, I offer special thanks to David L. Gearhart for his fine skill and support in the type-setting, and to the artist Goriam who collaborated with me in imagining and producing the drawings.

John Peter Sullivan
April 1998
Boston, Massachusetts

Introduction

Take off your shoes from your feet, for the place
on which you are standing is holy ground.
(Exodus 3:5)

Historically, the professional practice of psychotherapy has been dominated by a tendency to either ignore or pathologize the religious and spiritual dimension of human life. The early origins of the discipline of psychology are significantly marked by a movement to dissociate psychology from the more speculative discipline of philosophy and to establish psychology as an empirical science. The mainstream development of the field of psychology has been characterized by the diminishment or exclusion of the religious and spiritual dimension of human experience as a legitimate domain of attention (Shafranske & Gorsuch, 1984). The pluralistic, contemporary practice of psychotherapy largely finds its modern origins in the practice of psychoanalysis begun by Freud who overwhelmingly pathologized the spiritual and religious material of his patients and was highly critical of religion as an oppressive social force.

In an invited 1986 address to the American Psychological Association and in his book *Freud and the Problem of God* (1990), renowned theologian Hans Kung acknowledges that Freud and the psychoanalytic movement have contributed much in the way of a constructive critique of religion. However, Kung argues that historically psychoanalysis has demonstrated little understanding or appreciation of the healthy role that spiritual and religious experience can play in human life and psychological functioning. Kung claims that spirituality and religion remain repressed and in need of attention in the unconscious of the practitioners of contemporary psychotherapy. Gay (cited in Lannert, 1991) similarly holds that spiritual and religious concerns may well be the "last taboo" to be addressed in mental health care.

In their review of recent research on the religiosity and spirituality of the general United States public and of mental health professionals, Lukoff, Turner, and Lu (1992, 1993) discovered a significant gap between the religiosity but not the spirituality of the general public and mental health professionals. They refer to religiosity as "adherence to the beliefs and practices of an organized church or religious institution" (Shafranske & Maloney, 1990, p. 72). Spirituality is referred to as describing "the transcendental relationship between the person and a Higher Being, a quality that goes beyond a specific religious affiliation" (Peterson & Nelson, 1987).

Numerous studies and surveys reviewed indicate that mental health professionals place much less importance on religious beliefs and practices than the general U.S. public (Lukoff, Turner, & Lu, 1992). In their national survey of the religiosity of psychotherapists, Bergin and Jensen (1990) found that psychologists demonstrated the least agreement (33%) with the statement, "My whole approach to life is based on my religion," as compared to other mental health professionals (51%) and the general population (72%). Gallup (1985) surveys show that one third of the U.S. population consider religion to be the most important dimension of their lives, and another one third of the population consider religion to be a very important dimension of their lives. A similar disparity was not found to exist between mental health professionals' and the general public's valuing of spirituality in their lives (Lukoff, Turner, & Lu, 1993). While only 44% of therapists endorsed having a "religious affiliation in which one actively participates," 68% endorsed the item, "seek a spiritual understanding of the universe and one's place in it" (Bergin & Jensen, 1990).

While mental health professionals may value the spiritual dimension of their lives no less than the general population they serve, the literature demonstrates a lack of adequate professional training to prepare mental health practitioners to respond effectively to religious and spiritual issues as they arise in psychotherapy. A survey of members of the American Psychological Association indicated that 83% of those surveyed stated that discussions of religion in training occurred rarely or never and only 33% felt competent to address religious and spiritual concerns in psychotherapy (Shafranske & Maloney, 1990). Bergin and Jensen (1990) suggest from their research that because of the secular nature of most mainstream mental health professional education and practice and the significantly unrecognized though less conventional religiousness among therapists, there may be a largely untapped professional resource of spiritual interests among psychotherapists.

It is this largely untapped professional resource of spirituality that this study attempts to make more understandable and utilizable for the practice of psychotherapy. It is my assumption that, varying in degrees of personal development, the spiritual is an essential dimension of human life which potentially can be better utilized by psychotherapists to facilitate healing and growth. It was the intention of this study to explore and describe the significance of the spirituality of the psychotherapist as a professional resource for the practice of psychotherapy. The goal of the study was not primarily a theoretical integration of psychology and spirituality and religion, or to experimentally argue for the benefits of integrating spirituality and religion into the practice of psychotherapy. This study attempts to explore and describe how particular psychotherapists' experience their spirituality as impacting the way they work clinically. By focusing on the spirituality of the psychotherapist as it impacts clinical work, it was the intention of this study to illuminate, primarily by examples, how the spiritual and religious dimension of human experience can be integrated into and enrich the psychotherapeutic process.

Although spirituality can be understood in diverse ways, for the purpose of this study spirituality is understood as the actual lived experience of the person's relationship with God, the Ultimate Spirit, the fundamental life-force. Spirituality is here understood as characterized by mystery, that is, that which is not fully understood or understandable but able to be experienced, sensed, felt, appreciated, and loved (May, 1982). Spirituality is understood as at times inclusive of, but not necessarily limited to religiosity which is understood as "adherence to particular beliefs and practices of an organized church or religious institution" (Shafranske & Maloney, 1990). The terms "spirituality" and "religion" are often used interchangeably. However, the term "spirituality" does not necessarily mean affiliation with a particular religious organization. At the same time, a person may be religiously involved without necessarily being particularly spiritual. "Spirituality" suggests a broader and more personal meaning than "religion," although one's spirituality frequently stems from the religious context of one's life (Payne, Bergin, and Loftus, 1992). For the purpose of this study, psychotherapy will be understood as the clinical practice conducted by state licensed mental health professionals.

Through the process of semi-structured, in-depth interviews with selected psychotherapists who have been identified as models or experts in the research topic because of their exceptional spiritual maturity, the following central questions are explored: What is the nature of spirituality in the current life of the psychotherapist? What impact did the psychotherapist's spirituality have on their choice to become a psychotherapist? How does the psychotherapist's spirituality effect their view of who they are and what they are doing in their clinical practice? How does the psychotherapist experience their spirituality as providing a resource for facilitating the psychological healing and growth of their clients? How may the psychotherapist have experienced their spirituality as negatively impacting their clinical work?

CHAPTER ONE

Background: The Final Taboo

The twentieth century in Western civilization is unique in contrast to all other periods of cultural history in the way psychological healing and spirituality have been split within the public professional arena (Propst, 1988). The efforts of psychology to legitimate itself as a separate academic and clinical discipline based upon empirical science and the strength of the influence of Sigmund Freud in shaping the development of the professional practice of psychotherapy have largely given rise to this modern split (Shafranske & Gorsuch, 1984). Nonetheless, the diverse, contemporary systems of thought and practice within both the fields of psychology and spirituality share a common aim of helping to make whole the disintegration of suffering persons and communities. Both fields aim to optimize the quality of human life.

A multicultural survey of the history of the healing arts largely tells of the practice of healing by leaders in the community whose religious beliefs were integral to their methods and consistent with the communal context of their work (Calestro, 1972). Calestro (1972) emphasizes the importance for modern psychotherapy of understanding emotional symptoms of persons within the context of the local beliefs, norms, and lifestyle of the particular culture in which persons live. The contemporary practice of psychotherapy can be viewed as a contemporary Western manifestation of the long history of neoreligious and magical healing practices which have been a part of all cultures. For example, in many primitive cultures the religious shaman held key roles as both psychological and physical healers. Similarly, in the history of Christianity the priest or minister has typically served the role of psychological healer within the context of a religious world view shared in common with the community being served. The Christian history of pastoral care and counselling, or "the cure of souls" as it has been traditionally known, has utilized faith healing, meditation, prayer, the discernment of spirits, and confession as methods for both spiritual and psychological healing and development (Propst, 1988).

Within the current era of increasing social and political awareness and sensitivity to issues of cultural diversity, contemporary trends in the education of psychotherapists point to a greater emphasis on an appreciation for the impact of gender, sexual orientation, race, and ethnicity on the psychotherapeutic process. However, a critical lack of understanding and appreciation remains regarding the often central place of religion and spirituality in the development of clients' views of themselves and their worlds and its usefulness as a resource for the practicing psychotherapist. The re-integration of spirituality and religion within the contemporary healing art and science known as psychotherapy offers the possibility for psychotherapy to increase in credibility and effectiveness with the peoples it seeks to serve.

An Overview of the History of the Relationship Between Psychology and Spirituality

The early history of modern Western psychology during the last part of the 19th century is marked with a significant interest in the study of religion. As psychology established itself out of philosophy as a separate scientific discipline it was concerned with applying the methods of empirical science to the study of the religious aspects of people's lives (Wulff, 1991).

G. Stanley Hall, the founder and first president of the American Psychological Association (in 1891) and the founder of the *American Journal of Psychology* (in 1887), was the first American psychologist to study religion empirically. His studies in religious conversion are most noteworthy. Before traveling to Germany to study under the influence of Wilhelm Wundt, founder of the first psychological laboratory at the University of Leipzig in 1879, Hall already had received a divinity degree from Union Theological Seminary in New York and served for a short time in active church ministry. James Leuba and Edwin Starbuck were two of Hall's better known students who shared his interest in the empirical study of religion. In 1899 Starbuck published the first systematic work in the field, *The Psychology of Religion* (Wulff, 1991).

In 1902 William James published the classic work on the psychology of religion, *The Varieties of Religious Experience*. James was concerned more with a qualitative method of studying the religious experience of individuals using personal documents as case studies rather that the more quantitative methods of tabulation and statistical inference used by his contemporaries. His classic book appeared as the first significant example of a primarily descriptive method of studying religious experience (Wulff, 1991). (It is within this tradition of using a qualitative, descriptive, case study approach to investigating individual religious or spiritual experience that the present study falls.) In contrast to Freud, James' stance toward religion was much more positive. James' interest in religious experience was not in the philosophical or theological validity of religious belief and experience, but in the pragmatic, psychological function of religious belief and experience for the individual.

As the most commonly recognized forefather of modern psychotherapy, Sigmund Freud's primary emphasis on religion as pathological has had enormous influence on professional psychology's stance toward religion and spirituality. Freud studied religion extensively and understood it primarily as the neurotic expression of interpersonal and intrapsychic needs. His pathologizing position toward religion and spirituality is expressed in his book, *The Future of an Illusion*, originally published in 1927. Religion was seen by Freud as the product of civilization functioning to control, and thereby protect, humanity from the fearful sexual and aggressive instincts which motivate human behavior. Freud also viewed religious systems as the products of the unresolved, intrapsychic Oedipus conflict in which through religion humanity attempts to personalize the overwhelming forces of nature into a Father God. The religious concept of the Father God was understood by Freud as a way for humanity to try to influence the forces of nature and to cope with feelings of helplessness. This religious process was seen by Freud as parallel to how the young child learns to cope with the sexual dynamics of the parent-child triad. Freud viewed religious ideas as illusionary, neurotic wishes. For him "God" was merely a psychological construct with no objective basis in reality. The unitive religious experience of feeling a sense of oneness-with-all-things was dismissed by

Freud as symptomatic of a regression to an infantile narcissism in which there is a temporary loss of ability to differentiate between what belongs to the internal experience of the ego and what is of the outside world (Freud, 1927/1961, 1973).

Inherent in the conflict between the psychoanalytic movement originally driven by Freud and religion was psychology's investment in establishing itself as a science distinct from the philosophy out of which it emerged. For Freud, religion became the enemy, completely incompatible with science (Randour, 1993).

In the history of Western psychology, Carl Jung is commonly recognized as the great thinker in the psychology of religion, a healing bridge between psychoanalytic thought and religion. Breaking from Freud and his pathologizing approach to religious experience, Jung understood religion as integral to a healthy psychological life. In his essay, "The Spiritual Problem of Modern Man" Jung (1933) reflects on the development of modern psychology and psychotherapy as stemming from the inadequacy of traditional religion to give external form through meaningful dogma and ritual to the expressions of the human mind. He suggests that it is the task of religion to provide symbol systems and rituals which meaningfully correspond to deep psychic experience and therefore to serve as external social systems for psychic healing, transformation, and growth. He describes religious dogma as, like dreams, arising naturally from the collective unconscious of varying cultures throughout history in order to give expression to the numinous, spiritual, or religious experience inherent within the human psyche.

Commenting in his essay, "Psychotherapists or the Clergy," Jung (1933) critiques the theories of Freud and Adler as inadequate in their exclusion of the spiritual needs of humans:

> The kind of psychology they represent leaves out the psyche, and is suited to people who believe that they have no spiritual needs or aspirations. In this matter the doctor and the patient deceive themselves. Although the theories of Freud and Adler come much nearer to getting at the bottom of the neuroses than does any earlier approach to the question from the side of medicine, they still fail, because of their exclusive concern with the drives, to satisfy the deeper spiritual needs of the patients. They are still bound by the premises of nineteenth-century science, and they are too self-evident - they give too little value to fictional and imaginative processes. In a word,

they do not give meaning enough to life. And it is only the meaningful that sets us free. (pp. 224-225)

In striking contradiction to Freud, Jung (1933) understood authentic religious experience as an indication of psychological progress toward individuation, the process facilitated in psychotherapy and ongoing throughout the journey of life. Jung understood the goal of this process of individuation to be wholeness, rather than perfection. Individuation was characterized by increased access to and integration in conscious life of the healing and compensatory messages of the unconscious, largely from dreams, and a consequent sense of the meaningfulness of one's life. Jung clearly states the significance he places on religious experience for psychological healing:

> Among all my patients in the second half of life - that is to say, over thirty-five - there has not been one whose problem in the last resort was not that of finding a religious outlook on life. It is safe to say that every one of them fell ill because he had lost that which the living religions of every age have given to their followers, and none of them has been really healed who did not regain his religious outlook. This of course has nothing whatever to do with a particular creed or membership in a church. (p.229)

Arising from his experience as a survivor of the Jewish Holocaust during World War II, Viktor Frankl is commonly described as the founder of a third Viennese school of psychotherapy, "logotherapy." Particularly influential in the United States, Frankl's (1975) logotherapy is built upon an understanding of an unconscious spirituality as the primary determinant of human life. Frankl views psychotherapy as a process in which spiritual, religious, and ideological issues are regularly raised and must be attended to by the psychotherapist. He argues for a psychotherapy which is focused on existential concerns, that is, the client's "will to meaning" (*logos*) rooted in the reality of an unconscious religiosity and relatedness to God.

Gordon Allport's (1950) work in the psychology of religion is prominent in a contemporary historical account of the field. In the American humanistic tradition of William James, through his research Allport upheld an appreciation for the diversity of expressed forms of individual religious experience. An Episcopalian Harvard professor, his study of "religious sentiment" reflected his concern for the "soulless" state of much of twentieth century American psychology which had become dominated by a pragmatic behavioral perspective. With an interest focused more on conscious intention in influencing the future "becoming" of the individual rather than the classic psychoanalytic emphasis on the unconscious and the past, Allport theorized about the development of "mature religious sentiment" as an extension of general psychological maturity (Wulff, 1991). In his book, *The Individual and His Religion* (1950), Allport describes a central characteristic of mature religion for the individual as related to what the individual has determined for themselves to be of ultimate importance. His conceptualization of "intrinsic" and "extrinsic" religious orientations has been significant in the scholarly recognition of the multidimensionality of religiosity and has been instrumental in more modern studies in the psychology of religion (Ragan & Maloney, 1976).

Raised in an orthodox Jewish home in Germany and trained as an orthodox psychoanalyst, Erich Fromm (1900-1980) is a significant contributor to the mending of the early rift between psychology and religion. Similar to Allport in his efforts to distinguish genuine, "intrinsic" spirituality from false or lesser "extrinsic" forms, Fromm (1950) is noted for his distinction between "humanistic" and "authoritarian" religion. Fromm describes persons with an authoritarian religious orientation as projecting on to God all of their own most valuable human qualities such as love, wisdom, and justice and therefore impoverishing themselves in the process. Persons of this orientation are then only saved by self-deprecating, obedient surrender to a controlling, transcendent God. Because they are left feeling sinful and empty, they remain highly deficient in their ability to act lovingly in their daily lives.

In contrast, Fromm (1950) describes God in humanistic religion as symbolic of the higher self, the best of what a person should or may potentially become. The focus of humanistic religion is self-realization, overcoming the limitations of an egotistical self, developing confidence in oneself and others, and achieving the capacity to love and to respect life. Fromm notes the humanistic spirit present in various world religions and philosophers. His writings particularly reflect his admiration for Zen Buddhist principles (Wulff, 1991).

Influenced by the work of Fromm, Abraham Maslow (1908-1980) was another noted American psychologist well-known for his work which attempted to heal the historic dichotomizing of religion and the new science of psychology. Maslow (1970) is most known for his delineation of a hierarchy of human needs which must be met progressively, beginning with the lowest physiological needs, followed by safety needs, social and love needs, esteem needs, culminating in the highest need for "self-actualization". Maslow was especially interested in the characteristics of the more unusual, healthy individuals whose lives were motivated by the need to self-actualize, that is, to grow toward fuller knowledge of one's nature and higher levels of personal integration. Self-actualizers are described by Maslow as self-accepting, accepting of others and of reality, free from prejudice, capable of deeper interpersonal relationships, concerned for others, having clear moral and ethical standards consistently applied, creative, and experiencing an appreciation for the ordinary pleasures of life. Of particular note is the self-actualizer's reported mystical or "peak experiences" typified by feelings of wholeness, integration, relatively egoless union with all things, and full presence in the here and now.

Maslow (1964) described the human spirit's longing for transcendence common to self-actualizing individuals to be the essential core of religious experience though not confined to organized religion. Himself an atheistic Jew, Maslow pointed to a pattern within institutionalized religion of distorting, suppressing, defending against, and seeking to control the original peak or religious experience modeled in their founders or prophets. He envisioned that the peak experience or the intensely personal religious experience and the spiritual values associated with it would become more readily accessible for all, regardless of traditional religious beliefs or not, through the new humanistic psychology and the ultimate goals of all education (Wulff, 1991).

In the late 1960's in California, Maslow and other humanistic psychologists became the philosophical leaders in a movement within psychology that became known as "transpersonal psychology" (Wulff, 1991). Transpersonal psychology has arisen in an attempt to empirically study the spiritual phenomena which were seen as otherwise overlooked by contemporary psychologists. Carl Jung is recognized as a forefather of the transpersonal school of thought. Transpersonal psychology is open to the interpretation of these phenomenon from a naturalistic, theistic, or any other point of view (Sutich, 1969). As a multidisciplinary field it seeks for the integration of the whole person physically, emotionally, mentally, and spiritually, as well as social and environmental responsibility (Vaughan, 1993). Transpersonal psychology aims for the integration of Western psychology and especially Eastern religion with its emphasis on the practice of meditation.

Contemporary Literature Integrating Psychotherapy and Spirituality

Within recent years the field of psychotherapy has experienced an increase in scholarly research, theorizing, and publication in the area of the integration of spirituality and psychotherapy. This literature is noted for its emphasis on the potentially positive influence on the therapeutic process which the inclusion of religious issues and spirituality can offer (Payne, Bergin, & Loftus, 1992). However, in their review of the literature related to the "psychoreligious" dimension of healing, Lukoff, Turner, and Lu (1992) found in the psychiatric and psychological literature that religion was typically either cast in a negative light or ignored. These same authors indicate an increase of interest in the relevance of religiosity and spirituality to mental health in their subsequent literature review on the "psychospiritual" dimension of healing (1993). Within the contemporary mental health community, the pejorative connotation that is frequently attached to the term "religion" and the more accepting attitude toward the notion of "spirituality" is noteworthy.

Exemplary of this development of interest in things religious and spiritual within mainstream clinical psychology, the American Psychological Association's major clinical journal, *Psychotherapy*, devoted its spring 1990 issue to the theme of religion and psychotherapy. Similarly, Shafranske's edited collection of essays, *Religion and the Clinical Practice of Psychology* (1996) is a comprehensive work which addresses the religious and spiritual dimension within mental health and psychological treatment. The American Psychiatric Association's revised *Diagnostic and Statistical Manual of Mental Disorders-IV's* (1994) inclusion of a new "V" diagnostic code entitled "Religious or Spiritual Problem" is a small yet symbolically significant indication of the mainstream, American, professional, mental health community's recognition of the role of spirituality and religion in psychological health. In their article reviewing attempts to integrate spiritual and standard psychotherapy techniques, Payne, Bergin, and Loftus (1992) state:

> While research evidence is not abundant, traditional approaches are being applied to spiritual concerns, and spiritual thought is being extended into clinical domains. Caveats abound, but on the whole, commonalities are plentiful and rapprochement is evidenced where neglect formerly existed. (p. 171)

The growing magnitude of this theoretical and empirical research literature disallows an exhaustive review within the limits of the present study which focuses particularly on the spirituality of the therapist as it impacts treatment. An attempt will be made here to identify literature which reflects general categories of literature within this expanding area.

The rise in popularity of twelve-step support groups, an essentially spiritually-based program for recovery from various addictions and other psychological problems, has served as a substantial bridge of credibility between conventional psychotherapy and spirituality and has prompted an increase in this integrating literature. The work of contemporary psychiatrist and spiritual director Gerald May (1982, 1988) explores addictions and other psychological problems from the perspective of contemplative spirituality. May addresses addictions broadly as attachments which compromise human freedom and growth. His work explores the reality of grace, the power of divine love in human experience, as ultimately the only liberation and satisfaction for the human heart.

Propst's book, *Psychotherapy in a Religious Framework* (1988) is a key example of the literature arising from within cognitive-behavioral therapies which provides a practical counseling guide for including clients' spirituality and religious beliefs in the core of the psychotherapeutic process. This broad approach to Christian spirituality is written to appeal to both religious and non-religious therapists who work with Christian clients. The approach is directive, utilizing cognitive-behavioral techniques and theology in the treatment of anxiety and affective disorders. Jesus Christ is understood as the backbone of the therapeutic relationship, the ultimate source of healing. In their empirical study of the efficacy of the integration of religious imagery with cognitive-behavioral therapy with depressed religious patients, Propst, Ostom, Watkin, Dean, and Mashburn (1992) found evidence of the benefit of this type of integrated therapy for religious patients. These authors point to the significance of these findings, if replicated, for public health planning, given the religious orientation of the majority of the U.S. population.

Within the field of health psychology recent research demonstrates the effectiveness of behavioral interventions which integrate teaching spirituality to Type A personalities (Miller & Martin, 1988; Powell, Thoresen, Friedman, et al. 1986) and a significant reduction in coronary morbidity and mortality (Friedman, el al., 1984; Thoresen, 1987). The spiritual behavioral interventions of this research included teaching clients how to give and receive love on a daily basis, to view the world in a more cooperative and less hostile way, prayer, meditation, and planning time for rest and relaxation. Martin and Carlson (1988) advocate for the importance of designing health psychology interventions which connect secular prescriptions and proscriptions for health with the individual's and the family's spiritual belief system. These authors support a holistic approach to health care which includes medical, psychological, and spiritual methods for persons who are willing. In summarizing their reflections on the spiritual dimension of health psychology, Martin and Carlson state:

> First, the research we have presented suggests, in some cases quite strongly, that certain health problems may be related to deficits or excesses that might be termed spiritual, that optimal health may require spiritual as well as a social behavioral and physical homeostasis. Second, a number of health-improvement interventions can easily be characterized as spiritual, and these seem to have promising impact on the fields of health, psychology and theology. Third, health issues raise spiritual questions and matters that have been recognized for millennia. Fourth, many clients view the world and themselves through spiritual eyes and their behavior-guiding religious and spiritual arenas overlap nicely, especially so in health psychology. (p.102)

Arising from within the pastoral counseling movement, the work edited by Burton (1992) provides a resource for the integration of clients' religion and spirituality within a family systems therapeutic framework. This work describes how the spirituality of individuals, couples, and families can be utilized by therapists as a resource for understanding and healing family problems. Understanding and utilizing the family's particular "god-construct" is viewed as a critical aspect of the treatment system.

As a clinical psychologist working in Jerusalem, Israel, Spero (1990) argues that the most fertile ground for a synthesis of religious issues and psychotherapy has been found within an object relations school of thought, and to a lesser extent within existentialist psychotherapeutic approaches. He cautions, however, that a major obstacle exists still within these approaches to therapy with religious clients. Spero warns that psychotherapists will be obstructed in their facilitation of the exploration of client's actual religious experiences and religious object representations when these are assumed to exist solely as psychological phenomenon. He states:

> The assumption is that religious experiences and religious object representations ultimately point to mental activity generated by interpersonal (human-to-human) relations and discourse rather than to any objective relationship between humans and a divine object that in fact exists independent of human perception and language. While this assumption can be defended, it conflicts radically with the world view of most religions....The remnants of psychologism in advanced object relations theory of religious experience may confound the psychotherapist's ability to explore the patient's reality, such that the fullest value of paying attention to the central dimensions of religious experience may never be achieved and the unique relationship between the individual and the Object called God may go unexplored. (p. 54)

Echoing the same danger, Payne, Bergin and Loftus (1992) conclude that for the therapist to interpret all of a client's spiritual and religious constructs and experiences as epiphenomena, that is, psychologically derived and having only secondary substance or meaning, is to essentially disconnect with the client. Spero (1990) suggests that the widest extension of an integrated approach to psychotherapy which allows for the possibility of a "God object" Who truly exists would be one which understands psychotherapy itself as an expression or vehicle of a religious process. Understood as such, psychotherapy provides a way to help clients partially experience dimensions of the relationship between God and humans (Oden, 1967; Spero, 1985a). For example, through the person of the psychotherapist as a "transitional object" a client may be offered the opportunity to affectively experience divine acceptance and compassion which they previously may have ascribed only theoretically to God.

Similarly, from a Christian theological perspective integrated with object relations theorists, particularly Fairbairn, Benner (1983) proposes that the incarnation of Christ serves well as a metaphor for the role of the psychotherapist. As an *imago Dei*, created as are all humans in the image of God, the therapist from this Christian viewpoint becomes willing to accept and patiently bear the suffering, the negative projections and transference, of the patient. The therapist's entering into the painful and confused world of the patient allows the patient to eventually stop projecting their painful material and begin to integrate it into themselves with the empathy and strength offered by the person of the therapist. After considering various theoretical explanations for how the therapist's entering into the suffering of the patient in a particular way eventually produces change, Benner suggests that love may be the clearest explanation for this healing process. Benner states that

> love involves giving of oneself to another, making oneself available to bear someone else's burdens and to share in their struggles. This is not "sloppy sentimentalism" but rather tough, disciplined, and personally costly love. Its mode of communication is involvement. Its effect is healing. (p. 292)

The relatively new field of transpersonal psychology represents another sector within the growing body of literature integrating spirituality and psychotherapy. The practice of transpersonal psychotherapy places particular emphasis on consciousness as both the instrument and the object of change (Vaughan, 1993). This process is one not only of changing behavior and the content of consciousness, but also one of enhancing and clarifying the awareness of consciousness itself as the context of experience. Transpersonal psychotherapy places particular value on helping clients to recognize, understand, validate, and integrate into daily life their transpersonal or spiritual experiences as potentially healing and growth promoting.

A practitioner and academic leader in the field of transpersonal psychology, Bryan Wittine (1993) asserts that it is the spiritual world view and emerging awareness of "the Self" (a Jungian archetype which can be interpreted as the God within us) of the therapist that distinguishes transpersonal psychotherapy from other orientations, not necessarily the techniques practiced or the presenting problems of clients. It is this emphasis on the spirituality of the psychotherapist as the distinguishing mark of a transpersonal or spiritually integrated approach to psychotherapy that was explored in depth in the present study.

Contemporary Psychotherapists and Spirituality and Religion

In his extensive research on the role of values in psychotherapy and the relation of religion to mental health, Bergin (1991) states that psychotherapists are actually more personally invested in religion than would be commonly expected, although they tend to be less traditional in their practice of their religion. It was found that 77% of mental health professionals surveyed agreed with the statement, "I try hard to live by my religious beliefs," and 46% (as compared to 72% in the general population) agreed with the statement, "My whole approach to life is based on my religion." At the same time, only 29% of therapists rated religious content as important in treatment with all or many clients. Psychologists surveyed were found to be the least religious of the four groups of mental health professionals studied: clinical psychologists, clinical social workers, marriage and family therapists, and psychiatrists.

In their study of clinical psychologists' religious and spiritual orientations and their practice of psychotherapy, Shafranske and Maloney (1990) found of the psychologists surveyed only 18% agreed that organized religion was the primary source of their spirituality, yet 52% reported spirituality as relevant to their professional life and that 60% of their clients often expressed their personal experiences in religious language. Of the clinical psychologists surveyed, 74% disagreed that "religious or spiritual issues are outside the scope of psychology," and 67% agreed with the statement, "psychologists, in general, do not possess the knowledge or skills to assist individuals in their religious or spiritual development." As previously noted, in the same study, 83% of the psychologists surveyed reported that the frequency of discussions of religious or spiritual topics during their training to be rare or never. Meanwhile, as also previously cited, the 1985 Gallup survey reported that two thirds of the population of the United States consider religion to be the most important or a very important dimension of their lives.

Bergin (1991) points to a professional "religiosity gap" between mental health professionals and the public they serve. This apparent gap is partially explained by a significant lack of professional training in dealing effectively with spiritual and religious issues in clinical practice (Bergin, 1991; Lannert, 1991; Peck, 1993; Shafranke & Gorsuch, 1984; Shafranske & Maloney, 1990). Noam and Wolf (1993), as well as best-selling author and psychiatrist M. Scott Peck (1993) advocate for the importance of incorporating a religious and spiritual assessment as a part of any standard mental health evaluation. Several studies indicate that the attitudes and behaviors of therapists regarding how they respond in their clinical work to spiritual and religious issues are largely influenced by the clinician's personal beliefs and feelings about these issues (Shafranske & Gorsuch, 1984; Shafranske & Maloney, 1990). Shafranske and Maloney (1990) suggest that a positive correlation exists between the degree of confidence the therapist assigns to their own spiritual and religious belief perspective and the therapist's sense of competence in dealing with religious issues with their clients.

The lack of formal training in religious and spiritual issues in psychotherapy and the degree to which interventions are based on therapist's personal feelings about these issues raise professional ethical concerns (Henning & Tirrell, 1982). One ethical issue raised concerns psychotherapists working outside the bounds of their professional competence in their working with religious and spiritual issues with their clients. Secondly, the ethical danger is raised of therapists responding to clients' spiritual and religious material as an imposition of the therapist's personal views on these issues, disrespectful of individual dignity, uniqueness, and freedom of choice.

Psychotherapist's unresolved countertransference issues related to spiritual and religious issues can serve to negate or confound clients' exploration of these important dimensions of their own lives (Lovinger, 1984). The common avoidance of these issues by therapists in their clinical work encourages the isolation of this spiritual material and communicates to the client that it cannot or should not be an integral dimension of their therapy or even of their lives (Randour, 1993). Therapists are more frequently trained to attend to the bizarre religious delusions of psychotic clients than to listen for the implicit or explicit "sacred landscapes" which provide the ultimate context for every person's life (Rizzuto, 1993). Bergin (1991) notes the validity of a common perception among clinicians that religiosity can contribute to emotional disturbance, thus serving to maintain the rift between religion and the field of mental health. The well-known founder of rational-emotive therapy (R.E.T.), Albert Ellis (1980) argues forcefully that devout, orthodox, absolutistic or dogmatic religiosity is significantly correlated with emotional disturbance. Ellis suggests that the majority of contemporary psychotherapists are "probabilistic atheists" who view emotional disturbance as associated with the inflexible, absolutistic thinking which is characteristic of extreme religiosity.

The multidimensionality of spiritual and religious phenomena is critical to keep in mind in any consideration of its impact on mental health and therapeutic work (Bergin, 1991). Spirituality and religion offer abundant potential for personal and social transformation and healing as well as potential for destructiveness as witnessed in fundamentalist cult movements. Mental health professionals require understanding and skills that allow them to deal effectively with various life-enhancing, unhealthy, or even destructive forms of spirituality and religion, a central aspect of human experience. Moreover, the present study holds the assumption that it is the healthy development of the psychotherapist's own spiritual life which serves as the primary resource for the enrichment of clinical practice as a spiritually integrated process.

As suggested by Shafranske and Maloney (1990), it was my expectation for this study that psychotherapists who are spiritually mature themselves would express a confidence in their capacity to address the spiritual and religious issues raised by their clients. I also expected that these psychotherapists would view spiritual and religious issues raised by clients as integral rather than foreign to the therapeutic process. It was also expected that psychotherapists who are spiritually mature would understand themselves as facilitating not only psychological healing and growth but also the spiritual development of their clients. Additionally, I expected that how a psychotherapist described the impact of their spirituality on their clinical practice would be thematically similar to how they described the nature of their own current personal spirituality. Finally, I expected that psychotherapists would describe their spirituality as providing a strong resource for themselves and their clients which sustains and vitalizes their clinical work. I expected that this resource of spirituality would be understood as providing meaning, hope, and trust in the therapeutic process, particularly in especially arduous clinical situations.

CHAPTER TWO

METHOD

Rationale

In light of the evidence of the literature and my own personal and professional experience, this study began with the assumption that spirituality is a very important dimension of many people's lives which potentially can be utilized by psychotherapists to facilitate healing and growth with clients. It was the intention of this study to describe with depth and meaningfully interpret particular psychotherapists' experience of how their own spirituality is utilized in their clinical work. Given this research aim, a qualitative case studies design was employed.

The qualitative case studies research design allowed me to access the particular experience of each psychotherapist studied through the use of in-depth interviews. These interviews allowed the interviewees to describe in their own words their experience of the impact of their spirituality on their clinical work. The narrative descriptions from the interviews served as the data which was then analyzed and interpreted so as to illuminate for the reader a greater understanding and appreciation of the experience of spirituality as a resource for the practice of psychotherapy.

The use of a case studies design also allowed me to investigate with depth the experience of psychotherapists who are especially spiritually mature and therefore can be seen as experts experientially with regard to this particular research topic. The concept of "spiritually mature" will be explained in the Measures section where the screening instrument is described. The research participants who were selected to be interviewed are psychotherapists who by virtue of the depth of their own spiritual development are considered models for how spirituality can effectively be integrated and utilized within the psychotherapeutic process. By describing and interpreting the clinical use of spirituality in psychotherapy by some experts it was my intention to make the experience of spirituality more understandable and utilizable for mental health practitioners.

Selection of Participants and Procedures

Potential research participants were initially identified by a process of nomination by others in the professional mental health and ministerial communities. I solicited nominations through informal conversations with colleagues whom I knew to have a personal and professional appreciation for the significance of the research topic. I asked professional mental health and ministerial colleagues to nominate licensed psychotherapists within the state of California whom they identified as exceptional in their spiritual maturity and in their ability to articulate their experience of their spirituality as it impacts their clinical practice. Through this informal process of nomination, I compiled an initial pool of seventeen potential participants, nine women and eight men. Participant nominees were limited to those residing in California to limit travel time and expense. A pilot study interview was conducted with one nominated participant who consented to participating in the pilot study for the purpose of helping to refine the interview questions and the interview process. The data from the pilot study was not analyzed as part of the study.

An initial letter of introduction describing the nature of the study was mailed to nominees. This letter inquired about nominees' willingness to consider serving as participants to be interviewed for one 90 minute, tape-recorded, face-to-face interview with me. This introductory letter also stated that established criteria which consider the spirituality and gender of participants would be used for the selection of participants to be interviewed and that not every potential participant who willingly responded would be selected necessarily. Included with this initial letter of introduction was a four-item Lickert scale screening instrument (see Appendix A), a consent form which stated my intention to protect participants' confidentiality and the limits of confidentiality. The consent form stated my intention to minimize the degree to which a potential reader could personally identify any participant. It also stated that because participants had been initially nominated to be participants in the study because they were recognized to be professional models or experts in the research topic, their complete anonymity could not be ensured. The consent form explained that while particular potentially identifying personal information about participants would not be used (such as their name and specific geographic location), direct quotations from the interview might be used to illustrate salient points relevant to the research topic. The letter of introduction stated that within ten days of the initial mailing I would follow-up by attempting to contact by telephone each nominated potential participant to make personal contact, to ask about their level of interest and willingness to participate in the study, and to allow for questions and discussion regarding the specific nature of the study.

From the pool of all screening instruments and consent forms returned by potential participants to me within one month of the date of the initial mailing, six were selected to be interviewed. This one month limitation on response time for potential participants to be considered to be interviewed was set to allow the research to proceed in a timely manner. I determined that the six participants who would be selected to be interviewed would be those whose summed responses on the Lickert scale screening instrument reflected the highest degree of agreement overall with the four statements on the screening instrument. It was my intention to compose a sample group of three women and three men. I planned that if a close similarity existed among more than six respondents of women and men on the strength of each one's overall degree of agreement with the four statements on the screening instrument, the first six to respond would be selected so that the sample group would be composed of three women and three men. I also planned that if after one month of the initial mailing an insufficient number of nominated participants had responded to allow for a set of six, balanced by gender, the one month selection period would be extended until such a group to be interviewed could be composed.

Each of the six participants selected to be interviewed were then contacted to schedule an appointment for the interview in each one's office or in a private place of their choice. Before the scheduled interview appointment each selected participant was mailed a copy of the interview questions to allow for their reflection on the questions before the scheduled interview (see Appendix B). Respondents who were not selected to be interviewed were sent a letter informing them of this and thanking them for participation in this stage of the study.

Each scheduled interview began with a brief time of informal personal introductions between myself and the participant. Before beginning the actual tape-recorded interview, I stated again my intention to protect the participant's confidentiality by minimizing personally identifying details in the write-up and the limits of confidentiality, with the intention of freeing the participant to speak as candidly as possible. At that time participants were also reminded that they were free to decide not to respond to any question for whatever reason or to withdraw from participation in the study at any time.

I directed the tape-recorded interview by using the structure of the pre-established interview questions with the amount of time pre-allotted for each segment of the interview. I allowed flexibility in the use of the pre-allotted times for the various segments of the interview. I listened with interest to everything the participant said in response to each question, commenting with supportive remarks, reflections of understanding, and questions for clarification. My intention was to support the participant in discovering and articulating the nature and meaning of their experience in regard to the interview questions, while minimizing behaviors in myself which might have predisposed participants to respond in a particular way.

In the course of interviewing participants, several participants stated that they had no concern about being identified in the write-up of the study. One participant requested that their contribution to the study be personally acknowledged by using their name. Because of this request, after all the interviews had been completed, I sent a letter and an addendum to the consent form which gave each participant the option of being identified by name as a particular participant in the study. Four of the six participants who were interviewed opted to be identified by name in the original write-up of the study as my doctoral dissertation.

About two years later in 1997, in preparing this study for publication as a book, again I wrote to each participant offering each one the option of either having their name used in the presentation of their interview material or to have their material presented using a pseudonym. At that time I also gave each participant the opportunity to offer editorial comments on my narrative summary of their interview material. The editorial comments of participants who provided them were incorporated into the final draft of the narrative summary of their interview. Five of the original six participants gave their permission to use their names in the presentation of their case material for the publication of the book. One participant denied permission for his interview material to be used for publication.

Measures

Screening Instrument

The first phase in the selection of participants was the informal process of professional mental health and ministerial colleagues nominating licensed psychotherapists who are recognized as exceptional in their spiritual maturity and in their ability to articulate their experience of their spirituality as it impacts their practice. Further, I developed the Screening Instrument (Appendix A) as a way to increase objectivity in the selection of participants to be interviewed from the pool of nominations. The screening instrument attempted to evaluate objectively the maturity of each nominee's spirituality. Other than gender, spiritual maturity was the only selection criteria for nominated participants.

For the purposes of this study spiritual maturity is understood as the personal quality of considerable fullness in the development of one's relationship with God. While spiritual development is understood as a lifelong, dynamic process, certain characteristics of spiritual maturity have been delineated as important indicators of significant, adult, spiritual evolution. These delineated characteristics of spiritual maturity are reflected in the four statements that comprise the Screening Instrument. These characteristics were partially derived from Gordon Allport's (1950) description of "mature religious sentiment" and James Fowler's (1981) theory of faith development. Participants were asked to indicate the degree to which they personally agreed or disagreed with each statement as it related to themselves by rating each statement on a Lickert scale.

The first statement, "the development of my relationship with God/Other is a core value for my life," is rooted in the assumption that for the spiritually mature person the spiritual life occupies a place of critical importance among the various concerns of life, and that it is an evolving, relational process with God/Other. It attempts to evaluate the degree of importance which spiritual development holds in the individual's life. This statement is supported as an indicator of spiritual maturity by Allport's (1950) notion that comprehensiveness is one attribute of "mature religious sentiment."

The second statement, "my spiritual life relates in an important way to the major aspects of my daily life," attempts to evaluate the degree to which the participant assesses their spirituality as integrated into rather than isolated from the important aspects of their ordinary life. The assumption underlying this statement is that mature spirituality is not something relegated as a separate aspect of one's life, but instead is the dimension of human life which underlies and has considerable bearing on the significant aspects of ordinary human experience. This understanding is supported by Allport's (1950) contention that "mature religious sentiment" is not only comprehensive in scope, but also integral to the organization of a person's life.

The third statement, "the development of my spiritual life has been a high priority for me for a long time," was developed from the assumption that spiritual maturity is the product of conscious, ongoing attention to one's spiritual growth over a significant period of one's lifespan. In contrast, spiritual maturity is not understood as likely to emerge from a relatively recent or fleeting interest in spirituality. This statement is supported by Fowler's (1981) assertion that an advanced stage of faith development (specifically the fifth of his six stages) is unusual before mid-life.

The fourth statement, "I regularly participate in some form of prayer or meditation," reflects the assumption that spiritual maturity necessitates the practice of a spiritual discipline which sustains and nurtures one's conscious contact with God. This statement attempts to evaluate the degree to which an individual's spiritual life is not simply a belief system but is rooted in some regular, intentional, individual and/or communal experience of communion with God.

Interview Questions

Part I of the interview questions (Appendix B) contain four questions regarding professional demographics and four questions regarding spiritual history. The questions of this initial and brief (10-15 minutes) segment of the interview were constructed to elicit information that would situate each participant within the context of some of the particular details of their professional practice as a psychotherapist and of their spiritual and religious background. The information gathered by Part I of the interview questions serves as the professional and spiritual background for each participant, whereas the information elicited by the questions of Part II provides the core data of the study.

Having learned something about the details of the spiritual and religious background of the participant from the last four questions of Part I of the interview questions, the first question of Part II attempts to understand the current nature of the spirituality of the participant. This question attempts to situate the clinical impact of the participant's spirituality within the broader context of their understanding of the nature of spirituality in their current life more generally. Beginning to focus more specifically on the impact of the participant's spirituality on their clinical work, the second question of Part II seeks to understand what, if any, relationship exists between the participant's spirituality and their choice of profession as a psychotherapist.

Question three of Part II poses to the participant the specific, core question of this research: "How do you experience your spirituality as impacting the way you practice psychotherapy?" As the eventual focus of the interview and the entire research study, this question occupies the majority and remainder of the allotted interview time. This core question is further delineated into four subquestions.

The first two subquestions inquire about how the participant's spirituality effects their understanding of their identity and function as a practicing psychotherapist. These subquestions are based upon the supposition that the clinical impact of the psychotherapist's spirituality is significantly a function of the view that the psychotherapist holds of her/himself as a spiritual person in the functioning role of psychotherapist.

The third subquestion is rooted in the supposition that the spirituality of the psychotherapist offers to the psychotherapeutic process a particular resource for the psychological healing and growth of the client. This subquestion asks the psychotherapist not to theorize about the nature of this spiritual resource but to describe their experience of this spiritual resource in their clinical practice. By asking the participant for clinical examples of their experience of their spirituality as a resource for the psychotherapeutic process, understanding of the experience is hopefully further grounded and illuminated.

The fourth subquestion invites the participant to consider how their spirituality may have been experienced as negatively impacting or inhibiting the effectiveness of their clinical work. This question is based upon the assumption that the therapist's spirituality can be not only a powerfully healing and growth promoting resource in the therapeutic process, but that it also has the potential to limit or harm the therapeutic endeavor. Examples from psychotherapeutic practice are again asked for to illustrate instances in which the therapist may have experienced their spirituality as negatively impacting their clinical work.

The fourth question of Part II, the final interview question, provides the participant with the opportunity to comment about anything further that they may want to add before the formal close of the interview. This last question gives the participant the chance to further elaborate on some aspect of their experience or to give reflections on their experience that had not yet been stated in their interview. This final question also allows the participant the opportunity to reflect on their experience of doing the interview itself.

Analysis of Data

Each participant's responses to the professional demographics and spiritual history questions of Part I of the interview questions were used to create a background profile for each participant. The profile serves to introduce each participant with significant demographic and spiritual history details. Each participant's responses to the interview questions of Part II provided the material to be analyzed. The analysis of the data focused on answering the core question of the study: How do participants, individually and across all cases combined, experience their spirituality as impacting their clinical practice? The following steps were followed in the analysis of the data:

1. In the third person, I wrote a narrative summary of each transcribed interview. Each interview summary identifies the major themes which arose from each interview, using the interview questions to provide the initial organizing structure. Particularly salient interview quotations and anecdotes were included in the narrative summaries to illustrate major themes.

2. Each transcribed interview was read independently by one of the dissertation committee members. The narrative summary of each interview was then read by and discussed with the same dissertation committee member who read the corresponding transcribed interview. As needed, I edited each narrative summary taking into account the feedback of the committee member. Independent reading of the interviews served to ensure that themes which naturally arose from the data were established rather than only those themes that a particular reader might want to discover.

3. I examined all of the narrative summaries together and the core themes which were common to all or most participants were identified.

4. Finally, a discussion was provided of the core themes, the significant variability, and the usefulness of the findings of the data for application to the clinical practice of psychotherapists who are interested in the spiritual integration of their work.

CHAPTER THREE

Results

Of the seventeen recruitment mailings sent to nominated participants, eight were completed and returned to the researcher within one month of the initial mailing. Of these eight returned, three were from male participants. Each of these three male participants' summed score on the Lickert scale screening instrument was the highest possible score. Each had marked all 6's (strongly agree) on each of the four statements on the screening instrument. Each of these three male participants were therefore selected to be interviewed. Of the five female participants who completed and returned the screening instrument and consent form within one month, four marked all 6's (strongly agree) on each on the four statements on the screening instrument. Of these four female participants, the third and fourth female participants to return their mailing were returned to the researcher on the same day. One of these along with the first two female participants who returned their mailings were selected to be interviewed. One female participant wrote narrative responses to each of the screening instrument statements without indicating numerical ratings and so was not considered to be interviewed.

What follows are the narrative summaries of the five transcribed interviews of those participants who gave permission for their material to be published in this book. Each interview summary generally follows the order of the topics of the interview questions (Appendix B). Following the narrative summaries of the five interviews is a statement of the core themes which have been identified from the interviews which are common to all or most participants. The core themes will be elaborated upon in Chapter Four. There was also significant variability in the responses of the participants. This variability, including important individual themes, also will be addressed in Chapter Four.

A Greater Force That's Working:

Michael S. Hutton, Ph.D.

Dr. Michael S. Hutton holds a master's degree in East/West psychology and a Ph.D. in clinical psychology from California Institute of Integral Studies. He participated in clinical training and practice concurrent to the completion of his academic program. Additionally, he has received in-depth training in family systems therapy and spoke of the importance he feels ethically to involve himself in on-going professional training. He stated that he has been involved in the counseling field in California since 1977 and has been licensed as a Marriage, Family, and Child Counselor since 1986.

Dr. Hutton practices psychotherapy in two settings. He has a private practice in which he primarily sees families and couples as well as some individuals. He described his private practice clients as predominantly Caucasian and middle class. Previous to beginning his private practice, he worked for fifteen years in an agency with troubled teenagers from diverse ethnic and socio-economic backgrounds. In recent years he has also practiced with a small private group which serves couples, using as a basis the work of Virginia Satir and Harville Hendrix.

In terms of his theoretical orientation, Dr. Hutton described himself as a "transpersonal practitioner," meaning that he maintains a spiritual perspective in all the work he does. He spoke of the transpersonal orientation as an "encompassing point of view" which includes his systems practice with families, psychodynamic work with individuals and couples, and behavioral work as called for with families and individuals. He articulated the transpersonal perspective as not only assisting people in dealing with distress or problems, but also addressing such issues as "the broader reaches of human nature," where people want to grow, or struggles with the meaning of life as important aspects of doing psychotherapy.

In addition to practicing psychotherapy, for over ten years Hutton has been working as the assistant editor for *The Journal of Transpersonal Psychology*. He also teaches in the areas of marriage and family therapy, systems therapy, and psychotherapy with children at two different professional schools of psychology. He spoke of how he finds both teaching and clinical practice to be mutually enriching and growth

producing activities for him. Hutton pointed to the importance of his
teaching as providing a sense of greater balance and refinement to his
professional life as a psychotherapist, and seeing clients as challenging
his teaching to be honest. He spoke of his move toward teaching
psychotherapists in training as partly an extension of the sphere of his
influence. He also is involved in some professional writing projects.

In terms of his religious background as a child and adolescent, Dr.
Hutton was raised in the Presbyterian church. He described his mother
as taking him and his three sisters to church every Sunday, with his
father joining them only on holidays. He stated that he felt spirituality
was important to some extent in his family of origin, although it was not
pushed or discussed much. Regular church attendance was seen as
something that the children should do, but Hutton felt it was not
necessarily well-integrated into his family's life. He reflected on his
father's experience in World War II as having "jaded" his father about the
possibility of "some greater Being or wiser, compassionate Being in the
universe." He described his father's aversion to the possibility of God,
"that we were kind of all on our own," as having impacted the spirituality
of the family on an unconscious level. He spoke of his three sisters as
"not very spiritually oriented at all."

Hutton pointed to regular church attendance in his early life as
laying an important foundation for his spiritual development. He
referred to his memories of having profound religious or spiritual
experiences while in church:

> I had some experiences in church when I was young that were very profound
> experiences to me. I would call them religious or spiritual experiences,
> moments of feeling connected to the Divine, moments of feeling connected
> to God, moments of getting a sense of this connection with the community
> of people that were there, that I think really touched me at a very deep level.

As a teenager in the 1960's Hutton became involved with extensive
drug exploration which he understood as "a search for something more"
out of a sense that "something was lacking." As he became particularly
involved with the use of hallucinogens and psychedelics, he had several
intensely powerful experiences which spoke to him of "greater realities
at work." Not experiencing a place to explore these experiences in his
church, he drifted away from the church. He began meditating in high

school and turned to a vegetarian lifestyle. While in college he became more seriously involved with meditation and Eastern spiritual traditions which eventually led to his pursuit of graduate studies in psychology which incorporated some spiritual understanding. While in graduate school for psychology he also studied Hinduism, Buddhism, was introduced to Native American spirituality, and had a very broad exposure to other mystical traditions. He spoke of himself as presently having "come around a bit" to a strong interest in mystical Christianity as well. Hutton said he felt it was primarily his personal interest in spirituality which motivated and continues to propel his spiritual development and investigation of various spiritual traditions. Additionally, he noted the significant influence on his spiritual development of particular individuals he has known, including spiritual guides, leaders, or directors.

In response to the question about his current religious affiliation, Dr. Hutton pointed to the major focus of his current spiritual work as shamanic. He elucidated this focus as primarily "the connection with the earth." He participates in a lot of "journeying work," "sweat lodge work," and "vision quests." At the same time he holds up his contemporary interest in "the universality of religions," and "how they fit together."

In describing the nature of his spirituality in his life now, Hutton focused on his desire to make spirituality be part of his daily life all the time. He begins each day with a period of meditation in which his wife often joins him. He spoke of this practice as, "trying to remind myself that that's where I want to come from, everyday." He also stops what he is doing a couple of times each day to pray, meditate, or do some spiritual reading. He goes on spiritual retreats a couple of times each year either alone or with a small group. He describes these retreats as taking the form recently of "vision quests" in nature. Dr. Hutton spoke of making spirituality a component of all the classes he teaches on psychotherapy. For example, he stated in his teaching he can view the spiritual dimension as something as simple as stress reduction, yet he also understands it as something greater too.

I definitely think that there is a greater wisdom that encompasses all of us, that we're a part of, that informs what we do, if we let it, and guides, to some extent, what we do. For me the daily practice is to try to connect with that. It is not an easy thing. I don't necessarily find it easy at all. Turning back to prayer is sort of a new thing for me. It's really about remembering those points when it's time to express gratitude for small things that happen that I recognize are a manifestation, for me, of my connection with a greater wisdom, or God. That's important to me. And it's important to me to do that more and more. I feel like if I can be doing that then I'm sort of keeping in mind that I'm just me. I'm nobody great. I'm just me and I'm doing what I'm trying to do here in the world. And there's help if I just remember to tune into it.

Dr. Hutton described an experience as a teenager as pointing to an early sense of his spirituality moving him toward the work of a psychotherapist. Stemming partly from difficulties in his own home life, as a teenager he was instrumental in establishing a drop-in center for youth which continues to function today in his hometown in the Midwest. The center was established in a church. Hutton spoke of the church setting for the center, a safe place where people could come to talk, as reflective of his view of his spirituality as providing the basis for his choice to become a psychotherapist. In these earlier years, he came to see psychotherapy as a way for him to offer spiritual guidance in a broad context without being limited to a particular denomination. From his own experience of finding solace or comfort through "having a connection to some greater force or some greater element," Hutton came to consider that a psychotherapist could be someone who could offer spiritual connection or guidance for others. He stated that he never wanted to loose the spiritual origins of his decision to become a psychotherapist. Because of this he chose a graduate training program which included a spiritual dimension rather than a more traditional psychotherapy training program. He stated that his dream of becoming a psychotherapist rather than a spiritual director partly has meant, until recently, work with people with more severe problems, heroin addicts, chronic schizophrenics, alcoholics, and troubled teenagers, not "just white middle class people."

Hutton described a process of becoming less grandiose and more humble about his sense of himself as a psychotherapist through his years of practicing. He spoke of growing to appreciate more the complexity of the work of therapy and his own limitations in helping certain clients.

He has grown to understand effective psychotherapy as requiring more than good intentions. He understands his spiritual belief in the interconnectedness of life as having propelled him into the work of psychotherapy. He explained this belief in terms of the Buddhist concept of the *bodhisattva*, the ideal of living with compassionate devotion to assisting others in becoming awakened or enlightened as essential to the spiritual path.

In speaking of how he experiences his spirituality as impacting the way he practices psychotherapy, Dr. Hutton stated that besides the importance of the trained skills and abilities that he brings to his work, he also believes that there is "a greater force that's working." He spoke of this force as working through him and everyone. He described his understanding of the work of psychotherapy as "allowing that healing energy, that healing force to move through me and to be in the room when I'm working with someone, when I'm working with a couple." Because of this understanding he sees the importance of his having a meditation or prayer practice. He meditates before seeing every client as a way to clear his mind and emotional state in order to be as present as possible for each client. Although during a session he will pray in his mind for guidance or help if he and/or a client feel stuck, he stated that he does not meditate or pray with his clients.

While Hutton said that in his earlier years he saw psychotherapy as a way to offer spiritual guidance, he spoke of a responsibility he feels not to impose his spirituality on to his clients. He stated that currently he does not see psychotherapy as "spiritual guidance." Still, he believes that on some level of awareness clients are able to see who the therapist is and what the therapist believes because of how the therapist speaks to them or how the office may be set up. He holds the spiritual belief that each person must find their own way and so he does not introduce spiritual issues unless he senses the client's openness. He describes himself as helping clients explore spiritual issues when raised by clients, such as meditation practice. He lets them know he is open to spirituality, "not shutting them down around that," without directly suggesting a particular practice.

In describing how his spirituality affects his view of what he is doing in his practice, Hutton spoke of the staff training he offered as clinical director in an agency which served a very difficult teenage client population. Because burn-out was an issue among staff, most of whom had been trained "in more traditional psychotherapy schools," he offered training in stress management which included meditation, though not explicitly as a spiritual technique. He also facilitated staff reflection in making sense of their trying clinical work "in a broader context," though not necessarily from a spiritual view point, noting the importance of attending to one's personal boundaries and limitations as a therapist. Dr. Hutton described the danger of operating from "ego drive" in which psychotherapists can focus on how *they* are going to make clients change rather than on finding a way to allow oneself to be with clients, such as troubled teenagers, "so that they can experience the connection with somebody that will be therapeutic and transformative."

Dr. Hutton stated that he believes his own work with various spiritual techniques such as guided visualization has served to improve his intuitive abilities in his practice. He explained this intuitive ability as including getting a mental image or picture about a clinical situation which then facilitates understanding and deeper connection with clients. He described an example of this in his work with a young boy with behavioral problems and his parents who had unresolved issues from their divorce. Perceiving this young boy's difficulties as the result of being caught between his parent's conflict, in a family session Hutton received in his mind the image of the boy as a ping-pong ball. In suggesting the image to the boy and his parents he was able help the boy feel understood and his parents to see how their conflict was being experienced by their son. He also described using guided visualization with clients to allow them some experience of "contacting their inner wisdom, their inner teacher, asking for some kind of guidance."

Hutton indicated that his daily meditation practice is another important way that he sharpens his intuitive ability. He described his practice as in part consistent with the *vipassana* school of meditation in which he will take some time to close his eyes and simply observe his own mind, emotions and thoughts. This practice of just observing his own mind allows preoccupations, obsessions, or distracting emotions such as sadness to "shift" so that he can be more open and available to "intuitive flashes" and more sensitive "to how people are in the room."

Hutton stated that his own involvement with the shamanic spiritual traditions of Native Americans has made him more aware of "natural elements, natural spirits, animal spirits." He emphasized that he believes he practices psychotherapy fairly traditionally, using reflective listening, exploring the meaning for clients of issues they raise, and offering some interpretation. Although he does not initiate conversation with clients about nature, he has found that more of his clients are speaking in sessions about nature. He gave an example of a client who works in a stressful computer industry job who suddenly began to explore in sessions the meaning of the animals in the dreams he had been having. The client was curious as to why these animal dreams were arising for him. Dr. Hutton spoke of his belief that his own openness to such realms is communicated at some level to clients and allows them also to explore these realms themselves with him in therapy. He said, "I think at some level, partly it's because I'm open to that and my consciousness goes out and interacts with his."

Dr. Hutton stated that he believes his trying to be as open and willing as possible to explore with clients the material that they initiate in therapy is a very important spiritual aspect of the work for him. He explained this openness as helping clients to find the meaning for them of the issues they raise without prematurely interpreting. He spoke of this ideal of openness to clients' experience as a spiritual value which is important in working with clients who may have been alienated, abused, or traumatized through a particular religious affiliation. He suggested that his therapeutic openness may help such individuals to connect with a broader spirituality in their lives. He stressed the importance of respecting each person he meets in his office and allowing them the freedom of their own expression, particularly in the exploration of their own spirituality.

In considering the question of how he may have experienced his spirituality as negatively impacting or inhibiting the effectiveness of his clinical work, Dr. Hutton focused on two possible dangers he saw for himself. In the first case he spoke of his awareness of the possibility that he could impose some aspect of his own spirituality, his own belief system, on to his clients. He used the example of his client who in therapy presented his dreams with animals in a way which easily invited a shamanic approach to working with these dreams. Mindful of his own interest in shamanism, he wondered how he may have communicated to his client that he had this interest.

Is somehow some of my unconscious, some of the things that I'm interested in filtering out into the room? And are they picking up on that? Part of my spiritual belief is, yeh, when we sit down and talk together, ...our consciousness' merge, that they overlap and they start to impact one another and that you can't avoid that.

While he acknowledged his belief that he feels he is changed by working with his clients, Hutton stressed his ethical commitment to try to be aware of not using his work with his clients to address his own issues or spiritual interests. He spoke of this ethical commitment to increasing awareness of self, of how each of us has impact in the world, and of choices as an important aspect of his view of the spiritual path and of doing psychotherapy.

The second clinical danger which Hutton described as stemming from his spirituality related to his collection of full fees from clients, especially those who may be struggling financially. He explained that his own spiritual training has influenced him to want to sometimes give freely of his gifts as a psychotherapist. He recognizes that this perspective could contribute to his avoidance of the clinical opportunity to address payment issues with clients when they may be pertinent therapeutic issues. He relayed an example of this personal dilemma which he experienced when the check of one of his clients bounced. Hutton knew that the client had been really struggling financially. After he sorted through his own conflict about how to handle the situation given his spiritual value of assisting those in need, he recognized the importance clinically of addressing the issue with his client as it related to how the client may have been over-extending himself in his life in general.

To conclude Dr. Hutton spoke of his appreciation for this study because of his belief that spirituality is a crucial issue for the field of psychotherapy. He stated his view that in many ways the field of psychotherapy has been damaged by being cut-off from spiritual issues. He spoke of the challenges to psychotherapy in these times of managed care and government cuts in mental health services. In conclusion he stated:

I believe that there's an increasing sense in the population that they want to know about spirituality and they want to get reconnected to spiritual nature. And I think psychotherapy can be a bridge in that way to allow people to see that there is some greater meaning to what's happening in the world, that there's some greater forces, there's some greater powers, there's some greater intelligence that can be accessed and that can make living more interesting, or more enjoyable, or more growthful. So, I'm really glad that you're doing this study because I really see that as the direction that the whole field needs to go in.

Freeing The Self God Created One To Be:

Marianna Torrano, R.S.C.J., Ph.D.

Dr. Marianna Torrano completed her bachelor's degree in education and languages. She work for many years in education before beginning her graduate studies in psychology when she was in her late thirty's. She received a master's degree and a Ph.D. in psychology. During her graduate training she participated in clinical work in various settings, including a hospital-based crisis center, a school for young children, a Veterans Administration hospital, and a state mental hospital.

Dr. Torrano became licensed as a clinical psychologist in 1980. She stated that almost all of her clients have sought her out because of her religious background. As a religious sister, she has been a member of a Roman Catholic women's congregation for many years since her early adulthood. Most of her clients in the past have also been religious women as well as some priests. She stated that she has rarely had clients who did not have "a religious background that was explicit."

After earning her doctorate Dr. Torrano established a consultation service for religious personnel and worked more than full-time as a psychotherapist for many years. She set-up this center because she found that religious people were seeking psychotherapy and being left disappointed because they felt that their spiritual life was "at best ignored." She saw that there were conflicts, sometimes moral, between religious clients and psychotherapists. She described her practice of psychotherapy during this time as "traditional," being clear about not doing spiritual direction. However, she stated that she always was looking to see if her psychotherapy clients needed more than psychotherapy, such as spiritual direction, and would sometimes work jointly with a spiritual director. She found that in some cases this was very effective. However, she stated, "When a person is really psychologically damaged and struggling with that, they're in no position to do any spiritual direction. They need first to heal."

In the recent past she has shifted her professional focus more toward spiritual practice. She does continue to maintain her psychology license and when she is asked she does see a few clients, lay and religious, for psychotherapy in a consultation room at a retreat center. She also stated that people do come "just to talk to me," and although she feels she uses her background as a psychotherapist, she does not consider it psychotherapy. Torrano described her theoretical orientation as having evolved over the years. Currently she sees herself as practicing from a psychodynamic perspective, looking at the developmental aspects of the person and considering where they may have "gotten stuck." She stated that she feels she does best with long-term interventions and that most of her clients have been long-term. She noted that part of her way of working includes an assessment of what the person is really looking for, i.e. is there a need for a psychological healing? or from her spiritual orientation, is the person struggling, as all humans do, without a particular psychopathology?

Currently Dr. Torrano is living at a mission station on a Native American reservation. She described herself as officially unemployed, receiving no salary. She stated that she went to the reservation and asked the people if they wanted to have someone come and pray with and for them and that "they welcomed me with open arms." She described her current life as busier than it has ever been. She stated that she is not on the reservation to do a particular thing and that the description of what she is doing is evolving. Some of the activities which Dr. Torrano described as occupying her time include playing the organ, consoling people, saying the rosary at funerals, consulting with and encouraging the lay minister and the mission council to move forward, planting gardens, distributing clothes, and distributing Holy Communion. She said:

> But in my own heart, what I see myself being there for is to encourage and to be with the people...which is to discover their own strengths and to call them forth. It's an extension of being a psychotherapist, I think, because that's how I see being a psychotherapist too. It's helping a person discover who they are and to validate that and to help them reverence that and rejoice in that...and build on it. Build on it.

In addition, Dr. Torrano stated that she has begun to serve as a spiritual director and a retreat facilitator, new functions for her life. She described herself as being drawn more into this direction "without completely forgetting the psychotherapeutic mode, because I see too much interplay..." For example, she had recently led a retreat for over a hundred lay ministers in training who had addressed family of origin issues. She stated, "It was very, very wonderful, just to sense the presence of God there."

Torrano stated that she was raised Catholic and that her family of origin believed very strongly in the Roman Catholic Church. Two of her uncles were Catholic priests. She described her family as saying the rosary together at night and attending mass every Sunday and sometimes during the week. She stated, "Spirituality was extremely important." She also said, "Relationship with God was primary, but it was more structured growing up than I find it now recently." She was educated in Catholic schools where she received religious education from first grade through college. Dr. Torrano explained that for about the past fourteen years she has had a particular spiritual director, a member of her own international order, whom she describes as having been "enormously helpful in freeing me spiritually...more expansive." She described her spiritual director as having studied Hinduism very intensely and therefore offering "all the richness of the Eastern tradition."

When asked about her current religious affiliation, Torrano said, "Well, it's still the same. I guess it will always be. (Laughs) I seem to be quite content with where I am. Although, there are times when I question...some of the things, but that's alright." In describing the nature of her current spirituality, she stated:

> It is much more expansive. I think I am much freer with God. Perhaps it is also aging. That helps with that. The fears have dropped off. A lot of my fears. I used to be terrified of just about everything...God and people and everything else. I was a very, very shy child. At this point I'm able to speak of my spirituality in a way that I wasn't able to for many years.

She stated that she feels that her own freer spirituality is common to the other older sisters in her community as well. She described it as a deeper, more personal, less structured, and more intense relationship with God. The focus is more on being, an increasingly constant awareness of God, and less on the things she does.

Torrano stated that she had some awareness of her relationship with God since about age six when she also first realized that she really wanted to be a sister. She sees that her desire to be a sister went through various phases before she actually became one. She stated that she always viewed her vocation as a sister as having the sense of "belonging to God." This later developed into "a kind of spousal, biblical sense of belonging to God" and her best explanation of her vow of chastity. When she went into psychology she said that her vow of chastity was questioned. She stated, "I couldn't explain it because there was no understanding that it was a consecration in a special sense to God." She told of recently receiving a beautiful insight about her vow of chastity. Just before her first visit to a sweat lodge on the reservation where she lives, she spoke with a man who told her of his experience of fasting. He told her, "I fast. I do this because it is a way of giving my body to God. We have nothing else to give God, just our body. What else do we have to give Him?" Torrano described a deep resonance in her own heart with this man's words and currently the best explanation she has of her vow of chastity, "that relationship of complete gift to God."

In further describing her current spirituality, Dr. Torrano explained that her relationship with God is growing, becoming more intimate, more trusting, and more joyful. She connected this feeling "very much at home" with both the people with whom she lives on the reservation and with God. She stated that when she was growing up that she was taught that life was hard, and in fact, her experience was that "it was very hard." She spoke of times in her earlier life in which she "really really struggled. I was in darkness, terrible darkness." She reflected upon her own experience with depression, recognizing that sometimes a clinical depression may be distinct from or co-exist with "the dark of spiritual night." She stated,

> There were times in my life when I said, "God is preparing me for something, preparing me to understand human suffering." And I really feel that was a tremendous background for my becoming a clinical psychotherapist. All of that personal, interior suffering. And when you surrender to that you are surrendering truly to what God's gift is for you at the moment. But there's the sense of, "I can do this. I can hang on and I can be strong. I can do this."

Through her own experience of suffering Torrano spoke of the acceptance of pain as "the way you show your love of God...and then there came a point where the suffering broke through, when God broke through..." She also pointed to a shift that has occurred in her experience and understanding. She stated,

What I have learned since then is that one can surrender to the pain and accept it, but when one surrenders to the joy, it's a deeper intimacy...when it breaks through and the gift is not of suffering but joy...to surrender to that and accept it. It is not something we do, it is something that is done to you...Just say yes...And so I guess that's the shift that's happened...It's a very deep and intimate kind of...when the presence of God becomes more and more apparent...not that I always remember it...It's just amazing...Life becomes more and more amazing to me...and more and more surprising in a sense. Every place I turn is something...a new revelation...

In responding to the question of the impact of her spirituality on her choice to become a psychotherapist, Dr. Torrano spoke of finding herself being sought out to talk by other sisters in her community who were experiencing anguish and confusion. She stated,

I felt it really as a call. I recognized the gift somehow instinctively and I felt that I was really supposed to do that...in a very good sense. It was a joyous feeling. And so I did, tentatively and rather scared because, you know, who was I to do these kind of things?

These were the years, the early 1970's, of great change and turmoil in the Catholic Church after the Second Vatican Council. She indicated that at this time when the old rubrics of the Church had gone many religious people like herself turned to psychology as a part of their spiritual search. She found that some people were participating in sensitivity groups led by individuals who were poorly prepared to facilitate psychological work, particularly with religious people. She felt that further damage and confusion resulted for some people who participated in these groups. Torrano described herself at this time as also experiencing "a lot of pain," and so went to psychotherapy. She said that she found her own experience of psychotherapy at this time to be "helpful though inadequate." She explained, "I was always expecting, somehow, to be able to speak of the spiritual part of myself as well..." She said that her therapist, "didn't understand that real well." She recognized that other religious people were going to psychotherapists "who knew nothing about religion and were not able to deal with it."

After completing her doctoral training Dr. Torrano began offering psychological services mostly for religious people, including workshops on stress and depression, group work for communities, assessments, individual psychotherapy, and change of career consultation. With the suggestion and some prodding from a supervisor, she eventually established a corporation to respond to the psychological needs of religious persons. She commented that her becoming a psychotherapist reflected her philosophical belief that a person cannot develop spiritually as long as they are "tied up." She stated that she understood her gift was to assist people in getting "untied so that they could then take off the way we're all meant to be." Torrano again emphasized her work as a calling from God:

> I believe in vocation. I believe in God, you know, pointing the way for you, really calling you to something. I felt being called to certain things very strongly in my life...certain things at certain periods. And this was something I felt called to do. I felt God was in the call, that there was a gift God had given that God wanted me to use. I felt excited about it. I felt God was with me in the work.

Regarding how her spirituality affects her view of who she is in her practice as a psychotherapist, she stressed the importance for her of keeping separate the distinct functions of the psychotherapist and the spiritual director. She explained that in the past particularly when clients had become more psychologically well some would ask her to provide them with spiritual direction. She emphasized that she would always say no and refer them to a spiritual director. She refused to do spiritual direction as a psychologist because she did not see herself as trained to do spiritual direction and wanted to avoid the "co-mingling" of spirituality and psychology. She said, "I tried to be very clean about being a psychotherapist." She stated that she sees herself as a religious person doing what any other psychotherapist would be doing professionally, using the same ethical standards, training, and clinical skills, but "knowing that there is more than that."

She stated, "I'm more and more aware of the spiritual dimension of the person that I'm doing the psychotherapy with." She spoke of working with a clinically depressed religious person and watching for the point in psychotherapy when the person may begin to speak about feeling God's presence after a period of feeling the complete absence of God and of human understanding. She stated, "I'm watching for when that switch comes, in terms of the healing." She explained that she "wouldn't do anything with it, but let the person continue to explore it on their own...I would just listen." Dr. Torrano spoke of herself as a psychotherapist who is able to listen to and attend to the spirituality of her clients, allowing it to grow, allowing the person to speak about it. She sees herself as able to interpret clients' spirituality "in a clinical fashion," seeing the spiritual dimension as part of "a growth process" rather than necessarily as a "pathological process." She explained that with encouragement from her former staff, she grew to appreciate the value of doing not only a "strictly psychological" assessment of clients but also a spiritual assessment. She has found that a spiritual assessment, addressing the history of the development of a person's relationship with God and their current "longings for God," also helps clients to understand their psychopathology.

Although Torrano reported that her clinical work typically followed a psychodynamic "psychological model" she stated that particularly when working with a suicidal or very difficult client that she would also be praying. She elaborated,

> I often prayed to the God within that person...that the Spirit that was dwelling within would help that person over this, because... you know, you can always see very clearly what the client can't see yet, and would like to tell them, and you don't because that ruins it. But I would pray that the Spirit within would spark that insight. And I think actually that often happened.

She stated that on rare occasions she would also ask a client who she knew prayed a question such as, "What happens in your prayer about that?" Reflecting on this clinical intervention, she explained,

> That's part also of who we are as human beings. That's part of what human beings experience. Even as a psychologist you can do that. So in that sense, I think my spirituality would lead me to make some interventions if the person had a sense of God.

She acknowledged that her willingness to speak more explicitly about spiritual issues in psychotherapy has evolved through the years she has been in psychology. She explained that not only has she become much less reticent about her own spiritual life, but also the field of psychology has begun to explore spirituality and religion much more since the time she entered the field. She pointed to the development of the division on religion within the American Psychological Association and the development of the field of transpersonal psychology as indications that spirituality in psychology is "not taboo anymore."

Dr. Torrano explained her belief that clients' knowing that she is a spiritual person, "or trying to be," is itself a resource for them. She noted her belief that as her own spirituality has developed her clients have been more open with her in sharing their experiences of God. She can honor and validate these experiences. In this regard she stated, "We so unconsciously affect our clients." She stated that she has found that when clients are able to access a spiritual dimension in their lives that the healing proceeds much quicker. She spoke of this spiritual dimension partly in terms of "the readiness for the healing...the readiness to go beyond." She confirmed that her own attention to this readiness for healing within the client is a spiritual resource which she offers to the therapeutic process.

Torrano explained her view of psychological healing and spiritual growth as a continuum. She described a psychologically damaged person who may be cut-off from relationships. She expressed the challenge as the therapist to establish a relationship with the person by providing a comfortable and safe environment which allows the client to begin to unfold their story and for her to offer validation. She noted her experience of feeling moved by clients' stories and sensing that this empathy is automatically communicated, though not verbally. She also spoke of times of becoming tearful with a client as they spoke of something particularly poignant. She explained that in therapy as clients are able to begin to understand their experiences, how these have shaped them, and experience healing, "then the inner spiritual sense of the person begins to become more obvious and begins to be able to be externalized more." She pointed to the healing process in which the energy that had been consumed in trying to contain the pain and dysfunction of psychopathology becomes freed for healing and "the recognition of God." She sees the client then able to naturally "surrender to God...I don't need to say anything," and "allow the pain to fall off."

She encourages clients who may be experiencing a deep depression "to go into the pain and feel it...They realize it isn't going to kill them. And also they begin to see its rationale." Sometimes depressed clients have accused her of being sadistic for encouraging them to stay with their pain rather than avoid it. Dr. Torrano remarked that gradually clients may recognize how their pain "has serviced them and given them depth that they would never have had before." She sees clients as able to appreciate in retrospect the value of the difficult therapeutic road they have traveled and sometimes recognize God's presence and activity in the process. She said,

> They have a depth and a receptiveness and an understanding that they never have had before. And at that point then they can begin to see how God was working...to help them heal. If they're spiritual persons they will naturally do that.

Dr. Torrano described her capacity to closely attune to her clients, to resonate at a feeling level with them, as a spiritual resource which she has to facilitate healing. She spoke of this capacity as becoming engrossed with what is happening in her client, such as feeling joy or pain in response to what a client discloses. She noted the experience of clients' surprise at the "in-tuneness" of her interventions. Regarding this capacity she stated,

> I think we all have it. I know we all have it...It goes beyond my mind. It goes beyond what I know. It goes beyond my personality style because I deal with all the different personalities. And there have been times after a therapeutic session when I just have been, like amazement. Where did that come from? How could I have said that? This kind of thing. Because it just came naturally and without any, you know, particular fanfare. It just got said. You know, this kind of thing...it's just an in-tuneness.

Torrano stated her belief that therapists need to learn to become conscious about using their own capacity to attune to clients.

She offered a clinical example from her practice of how her spirituality had served the therapeutic work. She told of her work with a man who had suffered terrible abuse as a child. A point came in their work together in which this client spoke to her about a recent experience he had while in prayer. The man told of a "quasi-tangible" experience of God which moved him to feel joy. Torrano commented that because she had experiences of God doing things that are quasi-tangible in her own life, she was able to recognize and validate her client's experience with a nod, a smile, or some simple words of confirmation. She explained,

The fact that I've experienced it I can validate it. And I haven't known until rather recently that this is a very common experience with human beings...But the fact is that God has been one of the best kept secrets going. And we haven't talked about it. We don't talk about what we would call mystical experiences. Oh, can I be mystical? But it's what we're supposed to be. It's natural. It's not something that's extraordinary because we are spiritual beings. There are times when we touch that in each other. For example, we both come out with the same words at the same time.

Dr. Torrano continued by reporting that there have been times, coming out of her experience of spirituality, when she has been directive. For example, she has suggested that clients may need a spiritual director, asked clients about spending time in prayer about an issue, and asked about what God said when a client was talking about God. She indicated her sense that these moments in her practice have been very helpful to clients. Some clients have told her that these more explicitly spiritual interventions were some of what had been most helpful in their work with her. She said, "...there's that hunger at that point for God. And perhaps that's why people have asked me to do spiritual direction with them, because they have felt that even more helpful."

In responding to the question of whether she had ever experienced her spirituality as negatively impacting or inhibiting her clinical work, Dr. Torrano stated that she had not. She did describe taking "risks" with interventions that stemmed from her spirituality which broke from her original philosophy of not mentioning God or spirituality in therapy. For example, she told of her termination with a woman client who was in a very abusive relationship, had been very suicidal, and had a deep sense of abandonment. Although this client appeared to be estranged from God out of a sense of guilt, Torrano felt that she was able to connect with her spiritually "in a very extraordinary way...not religious in a specific sense." She described this intuitive sense of spiritual connection with this client as the reason why the client wanted to see her. Upon termination, she gave this client a stone communicating to her that she was praying for her, as "something to hold on to." Much later the client contacted Torrano and told her that in fact the stone had been what she had held on to, knowing Torrano had kept her in her prayer. In reflecting on taking such clinical "risks," Dr. Torrano said,

...that's certainly not something I learned in psychology. And it was an exception to my own rule...and I think we have to follow our intuitions.

When we've had enough experience, I guess, of working with people and we kind of have a sense...we know that our instincts are getting sharper and sharper, then I think we can do those kinds of things once in a while and pray that it's the right thing, because you don't know. But sometimes the risks you take are more valuable to your clients than being according to the books. But they have to be wise risks...

In closing, Dr. Torrano offered some thoughts she had previously written which speak to how she understands the relationship between psychotherapy and spiritual direction:

Both end-up being freeing experiences. They make one aware of one's inner most movements, passions, motivations, blocks, and so forth, in such a way as to enable the person to recognize and accept these realities so that they are no longer destructive, and to work beyond toward that which draws us most powerfully to wholeness. Therapy does this through bringing into consciousness one's currently operating unconscious feeling, one's repressed affectivity and related memories. Spiritual direction does this also through bringing into consciousness what is not conscious. But, here the material is not at the level of affect or memory but at the level of transcendence, the presence of God within oneself and the work God is doing and wishes to do in relationship with the person, the call to something beyond.

Secondly, both provide an external support and validation of the inner reality. As human beings we need this. When our inner reality is consistently contradicted or denied, we begin to believe we must be crazy. This is particularly important in today's cultural milieu where the external, material realities have become paramount and the inner reality is, at best, ignored and at worst ridiculed and scorned. In psychotherapy, it validates the self within by taking for granted that it exists, by affirmation and peeling away the trappings of the personas assumed over time so when the self is uncovered in all his or her naked beauty, warts and all, self-recognition, one is enabled to take the steps to self-acceptance and true self love which is the basis for all other relationships. Spiritual direction validates the reality of one's relationship with the Lord by encouraging articulation of this experience in the context of a shared understanding, His inner presence.

Third, how therapy and spiritual direction relate to each other is more, perhaps, a question of how the inner reality is addressed by each, relate within the person. (Because the question here was, how does the therapist and the spiritual director, how do those functions relate? And it depends upon how they come together in the individual.) One's relationship with the Lord encompasses and gives meaning to the therapeutic process because it is basic, in terms of the meaning of existence, to everything else. When the extremely taxing work of psychotherapy is seen as a means of touching and freeing the self God created one to be, one's relationship with God can be the motivation, or at least one of the motivations, for entering into the process, and a sustaining force seeing one through it. (And I've had people say that, you know, "This is so difficult. I know God wants me to do it, because God wants me to be whole...") The work of self-understanding supports one's spiritual life because it forces one to become more truly honest and simple, to be who one is in the here and now, directly, without duplicity or disguise. I think that being in therapy is a very humbling kind of thing. It puts you face to face with your reality.

While both psychotherapy and spiritual direction require a skilled person who is wise, experienced, compassionate, capable of listening without argument, understanding without judgement, and responding without possessiveness, each implies its own methodology. Psychotherapy, the methodology is free association, lucid dreams, memories, transference experience, and the like. These are used to uncover what has been repressed so as to bring to consciousness and therefore make available for analysis, redefinition, change, and closure, the destructively unconscious elements within. This process can also unleash for good purposes, powers within which have lain dormant and unsuspecting. I see these latter as the other side of what we commonly think of as destructive.

And the methodology of spiritual direction: meditation, spiritual input, the awareness of the Lord within, and one's relationship with God rather than exploration of oneself. This forms the basis of a shared experience between the directee and the director. This dialogue affirms one's ability to be in such an awesome and beautiful relationship and encourages the timid to accept his or her awareness of and pursue his or her desire for such a relationship that naturally flows into an increasingly sensitive discernment of God's presence and movement within, as well as God's tenderly insistent invitation to be both evermore immersed in Him and evermore at one in heart with the sufferings of others.

Walking the Labyrinth:

Alexander J. Shaia, Ph.D.

Dr. Alexander J. Shaia's academic training includes a bachelor's degree in anthropology, master's degrees in counseling education and religious education, and a Ph.D. in clinical psychology. He stated that the training for psychotherapy which has been most important to him has been acquired outside the work he has completed for his academic degrees. This training includes two and a half years in psychosynthesis, about eight years in sandplay, and about twenty-five years of Jungian studies. He stated that sandplay is a major focus for his work and that he sees a "great bridge" between sandplay and spirituality. Additionally, Dr. Shaia did two years of training in a pastoral counseling program which integrated the theological perspective of the clinician in their practice of psychotherapy.

At the time of this interview in 1995, Dr. Shaia had been licensed for about four years in California as a Marriage, Family, and Child Counselor. Before earning his doctorate he practiced psychotherapy for five years in another state. He explained that about fifty percent of his professional work is occupied with his private psychotherapy practice. In his practice he primarily sees adults, about one third of whom are couples and the rest are individuals. He reported that about half of his clients are church ministers or people who work in church settings. The other half of his psychotherapy clients he described as quite varied, including persons dealing with H.I.V., trauma, molest histories, and those coming for growth issues.

Dr. Shaia described his theoretical orientation as primarily "Jungian and fairly archetypal" while also using Self Psychology as an auxiliary developmental theory. Regarding his theoretical orientation, Shaia stated,

> The part of the work that's most interesting for me is imagery and my belief that the image is the deepest language...I like to follow the image and see where it goes...I feel that in following the imagery...it allows me to stay closer to the person's own psyche and the psyche's own innate sense of where it wants to move.

Shaia stated that besides psychotherapy the other half of his professional life consists of giving lectures, conferences, and retreats to church and psychological groups. He claimed that he sees all of his work as initiation, a theoretical base which stems from a spiritual tradition. He explained that he came to the field of psychology with an extensive background in ritual and liturgical studies. He stated,

> Everything I learned about change I basically learned in liturgical studies. I really came to understand that clinical psych was just basically talking about the process of change in the same way that ritual was. But at base, my first language is the language of ritual, and that's essentially how I understand psychotherapy as a modern day rite of initiation.

Shaia described the focus of the presentations he gives to church groups as "a psycho-spiritual perspective of initiation." When working more within the psychological community he explained that he "shifts the metaphor," focusing on psychotherapy as a ritual of initiation.

As the son of Lebanese immigrant parents, Dr. Shaia said that he was "raised, formed, steeped" in the Maronite Church, an Eastern rite Catholic tradition. He stated, "spirituality was very important, totally fused in the fabric of my family." He stated that his family of origin continues to deeply hold a spiritual perspective though it is now very different than his own. He reported that he was raised "in a world where spirit and matter were very close together," with a deep respect for dreams, ritual, and a folk tradition. He described himself as growing up in the world of his grandfather who was a folk healer who used incantations, ointments, and natural herbs to treat the local Lebanese community. Growing up in a tight Lebanese community within a large city in the southern United States, Shaia explained, "There was no difference between community and church community. It was one and the same." He emphasized the unity of spirit and matter in his family tradition. Traditions and rituals relating to the cycle of nature and the natural and liturgical seasons were very important events both in church and at home. He said, "I wasn't raised as a Western person," and explained that in the Eastern world in which he was steeped "the church community was my family community." The focus of every Sunday was the church community. He elaborated, "There was no question about not going to church. It would be like not showing up for dinner on Sunday. It wasn't a matter of theological belief. It was a deep affectional bond with the people." Shaia explained that in the Maronite tradition in which he was raised the emphasis is not so much on the sermon, catechesis, or intellectual belief, but on liturgy as ritual. He stated, "...it's body, it's gesture, it's sound, it's smell."

Considering the experiences which have been especially formative to the development of his spiritual life, Dr. Shaia spoke of his family and church community in the South facing a great deal of ethnic and spiritual oppression. Recalling the burglary of family members' homes and the fire bombing of his grandmother's house, he knew as a child that because of who they were and what they did that they were physically threatened. Referring to his family's ethnicity and spirituality he said, "to hold it meant that it could cost you dearly." He also recalled becoming "very politicized" in high school in the midst of the civil rights movement in the South. He pointed to this time as the first break with his family and tradition since he felt they told him civil rights was not his fight to get involved with while he felt that it was.

Dr. Shaia then reflected on his college years at a Catholic university. Although he originally thought he would major in theology, he found it to be uninteresting and chose anthropology instead. He spoke of a "crisis of faith" as he discovered the great difference between his experience as an Eastern rite Catholic and the Western Church's experience. While having to negotiate his own stance, he discovered that the form of his own faith was quickly becoming different than his family's. Particularly while studying the ritual and belief system of the Navajo and the Hopi people, Shaia found a great deal of validation to return to Eastern Catholicism "with some new eyes." He pointed especially to the theoretical perspective of Jung and his anthropological studies as helping him to reconstruct an "internal spiritual perspective." Shaia indicated that it was particularly his study of the Navajo tradition which began his great interest in rites of initiation, providing him with a "window" through which to view the archetype of initiation as evidenced in different cultures in different times. He explained, "...from the seventies forward, I would say that one strain of my spirituality has been widening out and understanding spirit as a rite of initiation."

Also originating from this period of his life, Shaia stated that his spiritual development has been shaped by his "wrestling with what it means to be a man, and then trying to bring that back to my early family roots." In this regard, Dr. Shaia reflected on his relationship with the Catholic tradition,

It goes through this wax and waning in terms of deeply knowing that I stand
in the Catholic tradition, but also realizing that what the institution knows
of itself today is a very small piece of its tradition ...I feel deeply Catholic
and yet the institution would probably look at me and say I'm not Catholic
at all.

He went on to speak of his affinity for what he understands as the
grounding principles which were guiding the spirituality during the first
six hundred years of church tradition. He stated,

In that way I feel very Catholic, in a very broad sense. I personally don't
think of the Roman Catholic Church today as very catholic. It's gotten so far
away from its own principles that it's like a parody of itself.

When Shaia is in the town where he lives he is involved with "an
intentional community" of people who "are all practicing a Catholic
spiritual tradition." He stated that he is not currently involved with the
Maronite element of his spiritual tradition.

In describing the nature of his spirituality in his life currently, Dr.
Shaia claimed that the metaphor of the labyrinth has become a central
image for both his own personal spiritual process and the work that he
does with his clients. He spoke of labyrinths as an image of life and also
of the spiritual life. He described his use of the image of walking the
labyrinth as a basis for considering questions about where one is in the
process of their life journey. He said,

Where are we in the process of walking the labyrinth? What movement?
What are we integrating? Drawing towards? Pushing away? Are we
coming into the center of the Self experience or are we moving back out
toward the world? I actually sometimes, as I sit with an individual, have an
image of where they are walking the labyrinth, which sector of the labyrinth
they're getting into, and how far or how close from the center, and what the
next turn or the double back is going to be, etc.

Dr. Shaia explained that he understands the labyrinth as an exterior,
physical form of the initiatory experience. As primary images for the
work of his own spiritual life and his work with clients, he spoke of the
labyrinth and initiation as interchangeable terms. He explained that
cross-culturally "the great rites of initiation have four movements with
doorways or passages between each one of the movements." He spoke of

looking to the movements of his own life's journey to assist him in understanding a client's life, considering which of the four movements they are in and what trials and obstacles arise in the various movements and doorways in between. He stated,

> I mean to say a spiritual path is to say the same thing as an initiatory path. It's always cycling around itself. Whether you think of it as labyrinth, or whether you think of it as spiral. It comes back to the same place.

Shaia added that the metaphor of initiation is also the form that is held by his intentional community. He described this community as gathering around traditional Catholic ritual practices "but just at a much more intentional level." He stated that it is a liturgical community that is focused not on just performing rituals but on the spiritual practice of meditation, reflection, the process of reconciliation by working through issues, the fasting, and the alms-giving "that truly make communion." He explained that this intentional community is both important to him and a tension. He stated that it is important to him now "to try to develop an intentional community that holds spirit." A tension is created because his work calls him to a lot of travel and so he is not home enough to be present to the community.

Shaia also elaborated the tension he feels with his community in terms of the third and fourth movements of the great rites of initiation. He explained that these movements are about how the community and the individual can bring themselves back together after having experienced an initiatory revelation or epiphany. He stated,

> How do you create a community which respects the individuation of the individual and yet also maintains some sense of bond and form with each other? Where does the individual bow to the community and where does the community bow to the individual? The third and fourth movements of the great initiations talk about the work that has to happen there. That's personally where my spiritual work is now. It's wrestling with community. How far can the community go in really honoring the integrity of the individuals? How far can the individual go in respecting the community's needs when they're in conflict with some person or individual?

Reflecting further on the nature of spirituality in his life currently, Dr. Shaia spoke of his "real growth edge" as trying to integrate a healed sense of masculinity and phallos as an essential part of his spirituality.

He stated that recently he has been exploring "the enormous devastation that was wrought on the male psyche" particularly through the first thousand years of the Christian tradition. He explained,

> It's unsettling and shaking up categories and I don't know where it's all going. But, that's sort of the growing, cutting edge of where I am right now, trying to bring back in myself or re-connect or heal the sense that the experience of phallos is really holy and an essential, not an auxiliary or an aside, but an essential part of my spirituality. I'm not sure where that is in my tradition, and I'm not sure how to bring it in. At another level, I'm trying to heal sex and spirit. Certainly in the Christian tradition and just generally in the West, spirituality for men has been a castrating experience. It's been a place you leave phallos outside the door rather than bringing it in. What does it mean to think of an embodied spirituality for men? What does it mean, an embodied spirituality for me?

In responding to the question of what impact his spirituality may have had on his choice to become a psychotherapist, Shai replied, "Everything in a way." He explained that he came to his work as a therapist out of about twenty years of working full-time in different phases for the Catholic Church. He was not ordained and served as a director of education and in other capacities. He explained his movement from church minister to psychotherapist in this way:

> I would consistently come up to this place where what I knew about spiritual development and what I knew about initiation would be shut down or denied or blocked by the institution. I wanted to find work where I could let the entire cycle of the process flow and where I could follow the psyche or the soul without categories and restrictions, and with a place where the experience could be primary and the dogma could flow from the experience. So psychotherapy became sort of a natural flow for me. I don't think of what I do here in this office as any different than what I did twenty years prior except that I have the incredible privilege of just letting the psyche do its work without limitation. Essentially everything I learned about this work I first learned in my ritual and theological studies and now sort of hang it on the cloak of psychotherapy.

Shaia explained that although while doing psychotherapy with clients they are using "the language of the West which is about feelings and thoughts and we're sitting in an office rather than a chapel, interiorly my perspective is that we're discerning spirits in a very sacred space." He noted that his work as a psychotherapist now is distinct from his previous religious work "in terms of the form and the language that I use, but not in the internal perspective or the experience that I have." He described this interior perspective which he holds while doing psychotherapy as the view that in all discussion of thoughts or feelings with clients he is helping them discern spirits. Secondly, he sees himself as hopefully enabling clients "to have a deep Self or soul experience which creates a new order or a new meaning in their life." He stated, "I'm watching as they go along the path for the necessary trials and obstacles that come up in an initiatory experience." He described his view that his clients are receiving clinical psychotherapy while he also holds the perspective that they are "walking the labyrinth or the path of initiation." Dr. Shaia clarified that for some clients the fact that the work of psychotherapy is very spiritual and a form of initiation may never be verbalized while for others it is discussed from the beginning or in the process of their work together.

In his work as a sandplay therapist Shaia described himself as providing a protected and clear space for clients to make images. Having become more convinced over time about the process, he stated,

> The images just spill out and lead one either down or up to a deep experience of Self and then out again to a reorganization of their external world. My work in that is to hold the space and to really watch and wait and trust.

He noted that he sees this process occurring both in sandplay work and in face-to-face verbal psychotherapy with clients, although words often obstruct or cover over the deep Self or soul experience. Explaining that he sees this process to be the same regardless of the issue or focus that the client may be bringing, Shaia said,

> Healing and awareness in my mind always stem from the deeper connection or integration between body, mind, and spirit, and that essentially the healing comes from the individual touching in some way the deep Self/soul. And that's not a one time experience in one's life. That's a many, many times experience.

Dr. Shaia illustrated this experience of healing with an example of his work in sandplay therapy with a client who came to therapy wanting to move on with life after a recent divorce. He described this client as receiving medication for depression and wrestling with the divorce with a great deal of bitterness, anger, and loneliness. In the course of weekly therapy sessions over a year and a half, this client occasionally would make an image in the sand. Shaia stated that what he saw happening in the sand was a going through a doorway out into a very chaotic place and wandering around. Finally this individual touched "a deep Self experience through the creation of an image." With this experience the client began to reduce and then eliminated the medication and found a lot more vitality to begin to date. The client also began to converse with the former spouse and began to heal much of the bitterness of the divorce.

Shaia explained his view that the creation of the image in sandplay is work that occurs in ritual space in which one enters spiritual realities in present moment time. Using the example of the client above, he stated that the client "wandered down and eventually found the Self space. Their hands created the image but their whole psyche moved into a place of meaning that was pregnant and alive with the gods and the goddesses." He described this experience as akin to the opening up of kundalini energy in which there is a great rush of energy which often is accompanied by a fair amount of chaos that needs to be maneuvered very carefully. Shaia stressed that the creation of a sandplay image is not just a nice picture to look at or to diagnose, but that it actually "brings about an internal reality." He compared it to Navajo sandpainting in which "the person that is going to be sung over is placed on the ground and the sandpainting is created around them." The person is taken back to the time of the creation of the world and they participate in it. He explained, "By touching the gods at the moment of creation they balance themselves in the way they need to be balanced, and then can come back to the world in a new state."

Shaia stated that while in his own mind he views the sandplay work he does as essentially a spiritual process occurring in ritual space, it is not necessarily understood in the same way or made explicit with clients. He pointed to the similarity between his view of sandplay work and his early religious tradition. Both focus on moving into ritual space with the use of images, metaphors, and symbols rather than an emphasis on discourse or an intellectual lesson.

He indicated that internally he holds the view of his office as a chapel. He spoke of the great care and intentionality he used in creating the office, "to hold what I know of my spiritual tradition." This includes such things as how the office is oriented in terms of the compass and what symbols are placed on which walls. He stated his belief that a sense of reverence is conveyed at some level to those who come into his office. He expressed his hope that in his office and in his work that there be no division between the physical and the spiritual. Alluding to one of the premises of most Eastern rite Catholic churches, he stated, "All is mystery that we just dance and play with. I think of that a lot here. I hope that this is a place that people can dance with mystery. It drives the intellect crazy."

Dr. Shaia described his aim to reverence his clients as seeking to find processes that are the least intrusive and which allow the client's psyche to move with its own pace, level, and direction. He stated, "I don't try to hold myself as the wisdom person about what the other person needs to do. I try, in a sandplay metaphor, to provide a space where the other individual can do what they need to do." He expressed his conviction that the deepest form of reverence is to convey to the other individual "that they know what they need to do much more than I do." In this regard, he alluded to the mystery of his not knowing "what the answer is," but having an overview within himself of the different movements without necessarily knowing the path the other will take. He said, "I try to be a good enough companion, dancing with the unknown." He indicated the greater ease he feels when working in the sandplay space with clients because there they "are fully engaged with their own process" without as great a danger of being pushed by his own process.

In responding to the question of whether he had ever experienced his spirituality as negatively impacting or inhibiting the effectiveness of his clinical work, Dr. Shaia spoke of the tension he feels of how to "hold the boundaries" given the difference between the spiritual tradition and the clinical tradition. Particularly in working with clients who are obviously on a spiritual path and are dealing with growth issues, he stated,

> I find myself in the doorway between the two traditions when it comes to boundaries and how to hold what's appropriate for this individual. I think that that's going to be a question that I'm going to wrestle with for a long time.

In considering this issue of boundaries and the wider current practice of psychotherapy, Shaia stated, "I think that we're very close to taking the boundaries to such a point that psychotherapy may get very sterile. I feel a lot like Ulysses being lashed to the mast on this one." He characterized "a straight-line clinical position" in terms of "never more than a nod or a handshake," and the position from a spiritual tradition as a move to a "side-by-side relationship" from a "face-to-face relationship." In light of this, he noted the significance of his practice of always sitting side-by-side the person doing the image in his sandplay room. He clarified that this issue of how to hold the boundaries is more of a question and a tension area for him than of his spirituality negatively impacting his work.

Shaia stated his preference for the term "shadow" rather than "negative" in further considering this question. He offered his perspective that a shadow side of his spirituality has been the "tension as a man between sexuality and spirit," and his certainty that this shadow has been in his clinical work. He explained that his spiritual tradition, including his family and culture, has not addressed a wide range of issues related to masculine psychology, sexuality, and spirituality. Because of this, he stated that these issues have not been in his own awareness, and so he has not been able to proceed with many of the men he has worked with to the extent that he now can because he is wrestling more with these issues. He said,

> If that's a negative, if some people would say that that's a negativity, I'd prefer to think of it just in terms of shadow material that I'm wrestling with now. I'm sure that there's another level of shadow beneath that when that gets integrated.

In closing, Dr. Shaia summarized his work in the following way:

> My work is about helping people create an experience of communion. Communion is creating that internal table where all the different aspects can come together and be fed. To come to that table means that a lot of reconciliation has to happen. So, what I always hope is the end product of the work is the interior communion, but that's not the path of the work. The path of the work is a lot of reconciliation. There's a quote that I often think of which is one of those light posts for me from Dora Kalff who originated sandplay where she said that her hope was/is that sandplay would help bring about a harmony which reconciled the opposites and once that happened we could talk about

an experience of grace. And my hope and prayer is that the people I work with at some level can touch an experience of grace.

The Magnificence Right Here Right Now:

Emma Bragdon, Ph.D.

Dr. Emma Bragdon holds an undergraduate degree in psychology, a master's degree in transpersonal psychology, and a Ph.D. in counseling psychology from the Institute of Transpersonal Psychology in Palo Alto, California. In 1995 she was practicing psychotherapy from an office in her home. She practices under a Marriage, Family, and Child Counselor license which she has had since 1988. The clients she serves consist mostly of individual adults whom she described as "pretty sophisticated" and who have already "done a considerable amount of work on themselves." Because she does a lot of traveling and teaching, Bragdon is regularly away for weeks at a time and so does not work with clients who may be in crisis or who may require weekly sessions. She states that her clinical work is "mostly with people who have issues regarding moving into their highest potential." She sees herself as having acquired a name for herself in working with this particular client population. Some of her clients are seeking follow-up work with her after participating in the courses she teaches. She stated that her clients tend to come from every socio-economic group. Regarding her clients, Dr. Bragdon said:

> They are people who have a vision. They see there is a way to move into union with their highest self. They want to learn to stop obsessing about some of the more mundane issues that much of the world obsesses about, either by conditioning or because they feel they have to.

Bragdon described her theoretical orientation as "quite eclectic." She stated that her "process oriented" style of doing psychotherapy has been particularly shaped by the training she has done with Arnold Mindell. Her extensive training through the Avatar® course materials has also been especially influential.[1] She described this training as not explicitly psychotherapeutic yet "highly therapeutic and extremely potent in terms of helping people move out of fixation and into liberation." Although she said she is not particularly aligned with any one theoretical framework, she did indicate an affinity for a client-centered approach. Describing her orientation she stated:

---

[1] Avatar® is a registered trademark of Star's Edge International.

I do not have a particular model of where someone should go. I help encourage people to reach into themselves, to become more self-aware, to get in contact with a vision they have for their life, whether that comes through visually or as a feeling in their body, or any other sense perception, to get in touch with something that we can generically call a vision and move toward that.

In addition to practicing psychotherapy, Bragdon reported that she is spending a large portion of her time teaching. For more than the past five years her teaching has consisted mainly of the Avatar course. She described this course as a nine-day intensive seminar "oriented towards self-empowerment. It gives very effective tools to help people into union with source consciousness, and become very deliberate about how they use their consciousness. It is about consciousness expansion and simultaneously staying focused on life goals."

Her writing in the past has focused on "the process of spiritual emergence" and the crises which sometimes accompany people's spiritual development. Currently her writing is focused on the interface of Western medicine and Native American medicine. With a Native American woman, she is writing a book which considers the importance of attitude for health, understood holistically, mind, body, and spirit, "the full functioning of the human being."

Dr. Bragdon claimed that although she was baptized as a child in an Episcopal church and her family attended the church, she did not consider spirituality to be a very important part of her family's life. She felt that her family lacked a strong allegiance to the church or church activities, and that church attendance was seen more as the appropriate thing to do. She felt that there was little connection between her family's church attendance and their home life with the exception of occasional prayers or hymns. She stated that she believed that her parents "didn't believe that they could have an immediate relationship with God. They felt very, very separate from God." She recalled that her mother, who had also been impacted by the Unitarian Universalist tradition, did a lot of journaling trying to understand God or the meaning of life but Bragdon felt her mother did not have a strong personal relationship "to something that we would call God." Spirituality or religion was discussed very little in Dr. Bragdon's family of origin.

Regarding her own spiritual development, Bragdon said that she began to meditate when she was 18 years old. This practice quickly became channeled into Buddhism. Between ages 19 and 23 she was closely affiliated with a Zen Buddhist community. For one of these years she was a resident in the community's retreat setting. She described herself between the age of 23 and 34 as being involved with the Native American shamanic tradition, studying with a Yurok Indian teacher until he died. At that point she began to explore a variety of forms of spirituality but stated that her "allegiance" is to both the Zen and Tibetan traditions of Buddhism as well as the Native American tradition. She stated that she feels there is a considerable amount of "crossover points" between the Buddhist and Native American traditions, although she would not call herself "Buddhist" or "Native American," in terms of taking on the particular tradition. For more than the past nine years she has done a lot of ceremonies with a Native American woman.

She pointed to her doctoral studies in transpersonal psychology as significant in helping her to think in a more integrated way about a variety of spiritual traditions and practices and their overlap with psychological development. Bragdon spoke of her experience while in graduate school of leading groups for women or focusing on female images of God or other deities as an important crossover for her in integrating her intellectual learning with practice which included ritual. She found that every part of her academic training contributed to her spiritual growth, particularly the deep personal process work that was done in a group. She stated that she believed her own personal psychotherapy contributed to her spiritual development "because it put me face to face with my relationship with myself, and my relationship with others, and therefore my relationship with all that is." She reported that currently she is not formally involved with any institutionalized religion, but that her "thinking is in line with Buddhism."

In initially describing the nature of her spiritual life currently, Dr. Bragdon commented that she had few words.

> I just got back from a silent retreat for a week, and I definitely felt that the silence spoke better than anything else in terms of the nature of my own spiritual life, and what I enjoy in terms of being in a position to go deeper into my spiritual life. To speak about it is personal, but that's not the

difficult part of it. The difficult part is finding some kind of words, because the words for me right now, even though I'm writing a book (laughs), the vessel of words seem so small relative to the kinds of experiences that I've been having, and mostly, look forward to the most, in terms of my own spiritual life.

She spoke of her spiritual life now as "definitely the most important part of my life," and "extremely rich." She stated that her spiritual life "informs" everything in her life. She understands her own spiritual development and assisting others in their own spiritual development to be what is the purpose and meaning of her life. Dr. Bragdon noted that she sees spiritual development as "definitely entwined with psychological development." She understands her "spiritual work" as noticing where she is fixated, where her energy is, since this may be what is separating her from what she calls "all that is." She stated, "I don't use the word 'God'."

Bragdon described her attunement to the spiritual aspect of life as having to do with "connection with nature and with something that is of the deepest sacred nature in human beings and in everything." The course she teaches assists people to "shape shift," shifting at will from identification with oneself as an individual human being into a deep connection and identification with others, i.e. a tree, a bird, the ocean, a cloud, etc. In this process a person's mind becomes very quiet and blissful and they are then able to gain access to a fuller understanding of their own nature and the nature of life. She stated:

> I found that kind of connectedness to be certainly a very sacred space. And as people get used to that level of connection they also find it easier to go into a deeper connection with themselves, into their own essence, and into a deeper bond with whatever is particularly identified as their own spiritual nature, as well as their own sense of what is most important for them to do or what they were born to do in this particular life.

One thing she tries to do in psychotherapy is to help clients to move into "the blissful nature" which is referred to in Buddhism and in different ways in all world religions. Bragdon said she is drawn now more to teaching, in part, because she has found that those coming to her for psychotherapy often have difficulty imagining that they could become so psychologically free that they could move into bliss. She said, "I'm most fascinated in that arena of human development where people gain access to that bliss, and how we can help each other and help ourselves into that state of mind." She described this bliss as giving herself and others access to deepening compassion and the desire to actively serve others. She spoke of this service as promoting a better state of health and well-being.

Dr. Bragdon stated that her own long-standing practice of Buddhist meditation and occasional Native American purification ceremonies help her to maintain this sense of deep connectedness and bliss. In explaining the integration of this deep sense of connectedness into her life, she said:

> It has become easier and easier for me to deliberately decide to connect deeply, let's say, with a tree or with another person, and to leave myself, my own concerns, my own thought processes aside for quite a stretch of time. One of the results of that is I have a pretty strong intuition or sometimes psychic capacity in terms of getting information on an intuitive level. For me the experience is more of putting me into deep connection, becoming part of what we could call "all that is."

Bragdon described her deepening capacity for connection and identification to also include a greater capacity for detachment. To illustrate this point she relayed a story of Ram Dass visiting with a despairing man who was dying of AIDS. She understood Ram Dass as having the capacity to feel the man's pain with him while also feeling deep within himself a level of bliss which served as a central point of reference. She spoke of experiencing more and more this similar capacity within herself, to connect with a variety of experiences while staying detached. She also feels free enough to allow for a relatively quick switching of attention.

Dr. Bragdon traced the spiritual roots of her choice to become a psychotherapist to a Buddhist vow she took at age 19 to follow the *bodhisattva* path, to help all people out of their suffering. She claimed that although she has struggled with this seemingly impossible vow, it has continued to stay with her. She believes that people's psychological suffering is much more painful than physical suffering. She believes that often physical pain is rooted in the psychology of a person. Seeing her own pain in the psychological and spiritual realm, she sought graduate training in psychology to help liberate herself and to eventually assist others.

Dr. Bragdon stated that she sees a great deal of her work as a psychotherapist is as a teacher. She sees herself as teaching clients by helping them to see, to validate and to make sense cognitively of their spiritual experiences as well as their current life issues. She may offer clients references to other people, other people's experiences, her own experiences, books, biographies, or films. Because she highly values the importance of learning to quiet one's mind, Bragdon said that she frequently will help clients to find a spiritual practice for themselves to assist them in becoming more detached from their typically turbulent flow of thoughts. She also reported that she sees her encouragement of some clients to develop more of a healing relationship to the earth or to animals to be part of the teaching aspect of her psychotherapy practice.

In describing how her spirituality impacts her clinical work, Dr. Bragdon emphasized the importance of being self-aware. She stressed her belief in the power for healing that can become available to clients when she as therapist is identifying with her own compassionate realm of consciousness. She illustrated this experience by telling of her work with a woman who had suffered a great deal of sexual abuse as a child and who struggled with multiple personality disorder. Bragdon spoke of the terror this woman would sometimes quickly switch into during their sessions.

> One of the most helpful things that I could do was identify with that realm of consciousness that we could call *kuan yin* or the goddess of compassion. As I moved into that realm of my own being to the best of my ability, I could be accessible to her in a way where she could feel deep connection and deep support, and not only feel that from me but begin to access that part of herself. My sense is that that is perhaps one of the potently healing things that can happen in a therapy session: when a person feels a tremendous level of acceptance and connection, deep connection, that does not in any way intrude on them, but, for lack of better words, gives them the space to be themselves, to express themselves in whatever way they need to.

She spoke of this felt acceptance and connection to sometimes allow for clients to experience a catharsis, to go beyond labeling themselves as "bad," "crazy," or "different" than anyone else and to feel more connected and whole. Dr. Bragdon explained that this level of therapeutic compassion and acceptance has become more important in all her work, particularly in light of the emphasis put on diagnostics in her early training. While she honors the professional responsibility of therapists to recognize clinical indications particularly of deep pathology, she de-emphasizes diagnostics in her work. She sees the possibility for diagnosis to be separating her from clients. In her therapeutic work she sees herself as trying to offer clients another view of themselves which does not highlight problems: "especially to assist them in connecting with those higher aspects of themselves that are more compassionate, and not so critical, and have more of a long-range vision."

While Bragdon sees her capacity for compassion as stemming from her own spirituality, she stressed the importance of the modelling of compassion which she received from certain of her own therapists and graduate school instructors. She explained compassion as, "the ability to attune with someone with awareness but not judgement." She noted from her own experience as a client in therapy the great healing which occurred, even in a brief moment, when she felt met and accepted in areas of her own life which were difficult for her to accept. She spoke of her appreciation for being with clients in such a way that allows them to unfold rather than attempting to fit them into a pre-conceived model of better behavior. Still, she claimed that at times in therapy she is very directive, such as in giving parents suggestions for improving interactions with their children. While at times she has strongly expressed the limits of her acceptance of certain behavior, she stated, "what I try to have in the background is that level of compassion and acceptance right here, right now." She claimed, "Generally speaking I think the compassion is the most important element for therapists to cultivate. Psychotherapy will definitely become a more evolved art and science as psychotherapists develop more and more compassion and wisdom."

Dr. Bragdon stated her view that the field of psychology and psychotherapy is still very young and unfortunately has been focused more on the study of disease and mental problems rather than "the study of human potential and the highest and the best in human beings." She said, "My spirituality has guided me into a much deeper understanding of what a human being can be or who we are in our essence." She has found ways to cultivate this understanding more through the spiritual traditions she has encountered than in psychology. She finds that the vast majority of the therapists who participate in the trainings she offers have trained their minds to look at what is negative or the problem in people before they can begin to see what is positive. She suggested the need to re-evaluate this common perspective among psychotherapists.

Bragdon stated that especially in the more recent years of her practice she has trained herself to focus on the positive in a person. She explained that she sees the positive as not simply what may be potential in the person, but "the magnificence right here, right now." She elaborated,

> To have that be what is brought forth clearly, that I'm enjoying and appreciating that aspect of the human being first and foremost. And then, yes, I will attend to the issues at hand. And yes, I will use my diagnostic skills and all the psychotherapeutic skills as well as the exercises from spiritual traditions in order to assist a person in coping with their issue. But, first comes more of the appreciation. I want that to be the backdrop and the most important part of the process that's going on with us. My sense is that as people work with me that they actually learn how to do that more within themselves, to bring out the more positive aspect that is already on-going, to bring out their appreciation for themselves just on an ongoing daily level. And yes, yes they have issues. Yes, let's realistically look at them and let's cope with them, but let's draw out appreciation for life too!

She described this experience of appreciating the client as something which she intends to communicate more through her presence than necessarily through anything that she verbalizes. She related this experience as "a feeling tone within myself."

> It's a feeling of lightness, enjoyment. It's a feeling of what an absolute magnificent creation we're living in, and what an astounding thing it is that we just get to be together in the present moment. And I'm truly feeling that. I'm not thinking it (laughs). It's not like a litany that I go through or anything. You know, we just get so accustomed to the day to day stuff that we all do. We tend to fall out of appreciation for just the magnificent creation that we're in. So, I attempt to bring that freshness back into human dialogue.

Dr. Bragdon illustrated this experience with the example of her work with a late middle-aged woman who has suffered with cancer for several years. She described periods of time in which this client has felt very drained, depressed, angry, and rather inaccessible. In her relationship with this client, Bragdon spoke of being able to be with her in compassion, fully acknowledging the difficulty of her situation while also bringing forth the client's "own joy in living, just the magic that is here." She found that often this client releases a lot of anger or tears which are followed by shared laughter and enjoyment. Dr. Bragdon stated, "So, there's a buoyancy that comes back into her life through relating with me." She qualified this by saying,

> I don't put myself out as a healer. I put myself out as someone who can accelerate a healing process. Maybe it's my ability to connect with nature and be more light. It's infectious (laughs) when you're around someone who is geared to that aspect of life, then it's catching, just like laughter.

She further named this aspect as "lightness" or "buoyancy." She confirmed the sense that it is her connection to this joyful appreciation of life which invites or facilitates her clients to access the same experience which is available to them. She noted again the challenge of putting words to her experience.

She spoke particularly about her own experience of "near death" as a resource she can offer especially to clients who also have had near death experience and are struggling to integrate it. Because of having spent about thirty years in her own spiritual development and her own traumatic experiences, "just being beat-up by life, meeting the hard edges of this world," Bragdon feels she can be a companion to people who describe near death experience or who go into altered states to tolerate pain. She believes she has less of a fear of death than most people. She stated, "I have a cellular knowing that whatever is on the other side of the veil is just a great place to be." She reported that she often gets feedback from clients such as, "I feel like you're with me," particularly as she has guided them in past life experience or visualizations during therapy sessions. She described her capacity to "almost participate in" and "experience the feeling tone" of what clients describe in their past life experience or in a guided visualization in her office. She explained that although not typical, she sometimes guides clients who are interested in past life experience. She focuses not on whether or not past life experience is "true or not true" but as a way to access personally meaningful symbols which are unconscious.

Dr. Bragdon understands her capacity to closely accompany her clients in their various experiences during sessions as closely akin to her previously discussed capacity to deliberately identify or connect deeply with a tree, a person, or some aspect of nature. Describing herself as very intuitive as a child, she recognizes that her capacity to attune to others' experiences has evolved. She explained this evolution in terms of her learning to quiet her mind in order "to listen to other aspects of consciousness that can't be heard because of the din of the thoughts that we usually walk around with." She sees herself as having cultivated this capacity to "move into more subtle realms with people," and continuing to develop it through the nine day trainings she leads almost every month, teaching others to develop the same capacity in themselves. Bragdon understands this capacity as a strong aspect of her life which she brings to whatever she does and which permeates her work as a psychotherapist. She noted that others have recognized in her that she has attained some peace of mind and access to a joyfulness in her own life. She believes that this recognition gives others the sense that they too are capable of living with such peace and joy. Dr. Bragdon claimed,

> I feel very strongly that if someone is going to be a psychotherapist or in the healing arts that they need to have attained some degree of happiness in their own life (laughs). I think we are put in that position of being models and that there are some people who don't take that on as an important role in psychotherapy.

In considering the question as to whether she had ever experienced her spirituality as negatively impacting or inhibiting the effectiveness of her clinical work, Dr. Bragdon stated that nothing immediately came to her mind. She considered the possibility that her own alignment with her own spiritual work or the spiritual aspect of her clinical work may inhibit her attending to clients' more basic psychological or material issues. However, she stated that she does not view human development in "such a linear fashion" so that a person's material needs must necessarily be addressed before one can address issues at the "upper end of the spectrum in terms of human potential." She stated that she receives feedback from others who say that she is "very grounded." Dr. Bragdon concluded by confirming her sense that in fact she has not experienced her spirituality as negatively impacting or inhibiting the effectiveness of her clinical work.

Dr. Bragdon is the author of two books: *The Call of Spiritual Emergency: From Personal Crisis to Personal Transformation* (1990) (currently out of print), and *A Sourcebook for Helping People with Spiritual Problems* (1992), available through Upper Access Books: 800-356-9315. She can be contacted by phone: 800-788-4084.

Death Rising Into New Life:

Margery Cunningham, M.A., M.F.C.C.

Ms. Margery Cunningham earned a bachelor's degree in philosophy and languages, a master's degree in theology, and a master's degree educational psychology/counseling with an emphasis in marriage and family therapy. At the time of the interview, she had been licensed as a Marriage, Family and Child Counselor for about twelve years. She stated that she was tapering off in her professional work. She was practicing psychotherapy on a half-time basis in a private practice setting. Ms. Cunningham described her clients as coming to her with a variety of issues such as depression, anxiety, and life transitions, particularly some older women in the second half of life. She stated that the majority of her clients are single women. She said that previously she worked for many years at two community mental health agencies with families and child abuse prevention. From her work in these agencies she has developed a specialty in working with what she described as "high stress clients."

Cunningham described her theoretical orientation as most influenced by her Jungian background and her training in family therapy. She stated that beginning over twenty-three years ago she participated in her own Jungian analysis off and on for about fourteen years. She stated, "It colors everything I do and think and feel." She also stated that she has read extensively in Jungian psychology. In terms of her training in family therapy, she said, "I never see anyone sitting here in front of me whom I don't look at as having his whole family sitting there, even though he or she is alone."

Besides her private psychotherapy practice, Ms. Cunningham volunteers with a program founded by a Catholic priest which provides respite and support for caregivers of people with AIDS. Through this program she provides up to three free therapy sessions with caregivers who are in crisis. Previously she volunteered for about eight years providing psychotherapy to AIDS patients, often doing home visits.

She said that she was raised Roman Catholic in a family of origin that was all Catholic and where spirituality was very important. One of her older sisters became a nun. Cunningham stated,

A swinging nun, I'd always call her. Kind of a very modern woman. Very artistic and interesting woman. She was very important in my childhood.

> She was five years older and she was very important to me...My mother was both spiritual and religious. My sister was too. Both those two were certainly the most important people in my life.

Regarding her family, she said,

> Almost all my relatives were deeply Catholic, in a wonderful way. They weren't slaves, though they all were very strict about their obligations. But they didn't speak of it in slave language. There was such a wonderful freedom about it. I thought it was a privilege when I look back on it...It's great to have a connection like that to the great traditions.

In describing the experiences which have been important to the development of her spiritual life, Cunningham said,

> I had a sense very early on of a couple things. To live and die well one had to spend a lot of time in prayer and make a relationship with God. And, that meditation had to be part of one's life and that one had to enlighten oneself in other ways.

She stated that in high school, college, and in the early years of her marriage she did a tremendous amount of reading "all the great mystics and spiritual writers." She said, "I was turned on to the great tradition and it was just such a gift." She also stated that she "had a wonderful spiritual director for many years, an outstanding person." She continued, "Spirituality just was my life. It was my life. It got me through all my life, and all these children, raising them, and difficult times and good times..."

Ms. Cunningham stated that she went to Catholic school throughout her education. She attended a Catholic college and besides philosophy and languages she also studied music and theology. She stated that after she married she had nine children within fourteen years. When her youngest child was a year old she began a master's degree in theology. She completed the degree in theology over a period of about five years and then taught theology and world religions at a Catholic girls' high school. She studied Hinduism and Buddhism and practiced a lot of yoga and all kinds of meditation. She described her interest in investigating other religions, including her travels through Southeast Asia and China. She said, "I saw these religions alive and it was very, very fascinating and interesting. And, I'm still convinced...I'm where I belong, though I love all those manifestations of God in other places..."

Regarding her religious affiliation, she said, "I was raised a Roman Catholic and I still am a Roman Catholic, though perhaps a different breed. I have remained terribly true to my religion in my own fashion." She stated that she prefers going to a church "that's a little more liberal" where the details of rubrics are not emphasized. She said she believes one has to believe "a core set of things...to be religiously affiliated...but it doesn't have to be thousands."

In describing the nature of her spirituality in her life now, Cunningham referred to Jung's notion that the great religious questions arise more in the second half of life. She suggested that the work of generating the major work and relationships of her life has already occurred in her past. As the mother of nine children, eight of whom are living, she is now a grandmother to many grandchildren. In terms of her spirituality she said, "I peaked very early, I think. I did a lot of my deepest, deepest meditation and spirituality when I had young children." She spoke of doing "serious, deep meditation" when her children were napping. Looking back to these years and then to her life presently, Cunningham reflected,

> It was fueled by this dynamic, from what I perceived to be God working and my connection with Him. So, it seemed easy. I think I've changed in a way. I try to meditate. It's harder now. It seems so much harder. I think that's partly the second half of life where I think that there's something different about this phase of life. You're seeing the ending of what you've done. And I think there's sadness. And there's happiness. But, there's sadness that, you know, things are coming to an end. You can't go back and change things. And so spirituality has a different tone.

Contrasting her spiritual life when she was a young mother to the present, she said she currently feels less motivated to read theology or spiritual reading and has no spiritual director. She explained that she is involved in a peer women's group that meets for various weekends throughout the year to "discuss serious issues." She said, "It's wonderful." She is also involved in a prayer group that meets in the seasons before Christmas and Easter. She stated,

I think that one needs a lot of support to keep the spiritual life going in the way you want. So, you have to work at these things. Meditation every day, Bible reading, or something. You have to keep that going. It's too easy to give it up. I have to struggle against weaknesses of all kinds, even after all my years. So, I think I, in a way, peaked terribly early. A lot of people are just finding spirituality now, and I've done it. So, for me it's really a thing of discipline. It's hard, really hard.

In reflecting on the question of the impact of her spirituality on her choice to become a psychotherapist, Cunningham spoke of several influences: the healing and nurturing aspect of the work, her admiration of a few good friends who were therapists, and her own Jungian analysis with a Jewish analyst who she described as "extremely spiritual." She said that as a middle-aged woman she made the decision quickly to give up teaching and to become a therapist. She said, "It was there inside of me, I think." She explained, "But directly, did I think because of my spiritual life I'm going to go out and be a therapist? I don't know. I mean, I was who I was and my whole being came into the decision."

Ms. Cunningham also spoke of the influence of her family in choosing to be in a helping profession. She explained that besides having a sister who became a nun, her brother was a doctor, and her mother was known for her hospitality to beggars. She spoke of her mother as providing a "gorgeous lunch" with an ironed napkin to beggars who came to their door. She recalled her mother saying, "That's Christ. That's Jesus out there. I'm going to give him a good napkin." She explained that although career options were not emphasized for women when she was a young woman, she did believe her spirituality did inform her decision to be a therapist later in her life. She said, "I guess my spirituality really said go and help, you know, and do this, all of this." She spoke of donating her service in agencies where she was paid nothing or very poorly. She said, "But, you know, you loved and you did it. And I did consider it a service, out of love. That came from my soul." Reflecting on her choice to do this work, she concluded,

They're part and parcel of our being, our choices. That's my view. That's my bottom line. They express who we are and who we have been. That's what it's all about. You don't make these choices out of a vacuum.

In answering how she sees her spirituality as impacting her view of who she is in her practice of psychotherapy, Cunningham said, "I bring who I am, the person you see. That's who I bring to my clients. I bring a life. I bring a long life experience to my clients. You bring who you are besides your skills." She stated that her life experience and her exposure to all kinds of religions has taught her "tremendous respect for people." She illustrated her experience of respect with an example from her work with her own therapist. She explained that on a certain occasion she was dealing with a lot of "dark and shadow" material in her own therapy and commented with some amazement to her therapist about how easy and gentle he was being toward her. Her therapist responded with amazement that she would ask such a question and asked, "Why should I abuse you?" Cunningham recalled that many years later she had a client who had had a very difficult life say the same thing to her that she had said to her therapist. She recalled responding to this client as her own therapist had to her, "Why should I hurt you? You're not here to be hurt by me." Reflecting on her experience with this client, she said, "I think that his transformation, if indeed it was such a thing, came about because of that deep respect that came across." She elaborated on this experience of respect:

> I think it's like Buddha compassion. I don't think you can get that when you're two years or five years old, or twenty. I think it takes a lifetime really. That's what the Buddha ended up with, that tremendous compassion. I don't have anything like that. I mean, I'm not the Buddha, but, I'm talking about a certain feeling and I think it comes with experience and age and looking around a lot and watching, watching, looking around at people. Living a lot.

She said that she finds it rare when a client does not raise a spiritual subject. Although clients may not use the term "spiritual" with her, she finds they talk about "something transcendent, something bigger than themselves." She said that although typically in therapy clients are working on their problems and issues such as relationships, depression, anxiety, and loss, she finds that "the underpinnings" of spirituality and transformation are present. Cunningham stated that she thinks she does not have the right and will not initiate spiritual subjects with her clients or impose her religious views on to anyone. However, she stated that she will pursue a spiritual lead or "any small clue" initiated by a client. She stated, "They're helped more if they can get the bigger picture." She said, "I always see where they are and what their position is themselves and how we can enhance and make it usable for them." She noted her

experience with elderly clients who sometimes come to her never having
thought about the spiritual life and frightened of death. She spoke of this
as a great opportunity to talk with these clients about where the meaning
is in their lives and how they could develop that if they wanted. She said,

> Always taking the lead from the client. It's not my job to force anything. It's
> my job to help enhance what's there. Help it grow. Help to transform it.
> But they have to do all that. I cannot do that.

Ms. Cunningham explained that she will suggest spiritual or relaxation
practices such as meditation or yoga to her clients.

She said there was a time in her practice when she was feeling like
a healer, although she never said so to anyone. She explained that she
no longer thinks of herself in that way. Instead, she said, "I think of
myself as a medium through which wounded people can be released of
some pain and grow. I'm not in there so much." She said that contrary
to the Freudian notion that the therapeutic work happens through the
relationship with the therapist, her view is more of the client having to
do the work. In this regard, Cunningham said,

> I think I present my being to my client and they take it or leave it. I mean,
> this is who I am. I am totally honest and totally present, and I am who I
> have developed into. And, I have worked really hard at that for a lifetime.
> I don't think about it anymore. It's just, here I am. And whatever happens
> happens. It seems to work fairly decently most of the time.

She stated that she believes her clients perceive her as a spiritual
person. She said, "I think it must come across." She noted that recently
several clients have commented that there is an "integrity" in her work
with them that they can trust. She noted that she thought the same way
about her own therapist. She said of him, "I've never met anybody with
such integrity." She stated her sense that her honesty, carefulness, ethics,
and her boundaries in her practice stem from her spirituality and are
perceived as such by her clients. She said that she tries to keep good
boundaries in what she reveals about herself to her clients. She
explained, for example, that she will sometimes talk about her experience
raising children and her knowledge from doing parent education for
many years, especially with clients who have children. She stated that
some clients do know something about her spiritual background.

In answering the question of how she experiences her spirituality as providing a resource for the healing and growth of her clients, Cunningham focused on meaning, transformation, and transcendence. She explained that within herself is the resource of spirituality waiting and ready to assist clients. She acknowledged her wish for her clients and for all people to be "connected" and to see "the importance of the transcendent." She stated that from her own experience her bias is that "people do psychologically better if they have a sense of meaning in their lives and they are connected to something other than themselves." She stated that this can take many different forms, one of which she has seen in clients is their desire to live a moral or ethical life. Although clients may not use these terms, she understands clients' wanting to live a good life by whatever ethical or moral perspective they hold as a way of their "connecting with something greater than themselves." She commented that whether or not clients believe in God is not something she asks and "isn't a big concern."

Cunningham noted her belief that the Jungian sense of raising one's consciousness about everything, particularly of who we are, how we act, and how we present ourselves in the world is "a spiritual calling." She said,

> I think it's a moral imperative almost, that we take every chance to be enlightened and to use that. I believe that and I've said that to clients that can bear it. I think it just wouldn't go over with some people. I think we are called to do that, to be more conscious.

She explained that consciousness becomes an archetype or a way to access "our deepest centers," or the "more spiritual self."

Ms. Cunningham spoke of the importance of thinking about clients in terms of the great Jungian archetypes of meaning and transformation. She noted that she sees a lack of meaning in some clients. She offered the example of an older woman client who was not connected with her religion and in some sessions expressed a fear of death, raising issues about the meaning of life. Cunningham pointed to her own spirituality as enabling her to discuss issues of meaning and transformation with her client. She explained that her client struggled to find meaning in her life and eventually came to her own resolution to begin meditating again.

Cunningham described this quiet meditative time as "a transcendent time. It's a looking to the Great Other rather than inward."

Cunningham referred to transformation as "a burning and purging and meeting the darkness and then rising up to the light." She pointed to Easter and myths of the Mideast as archetypes of transformation, "darkness to light movements." Regarding Easter, she said, "Easter was always one of the greatest for me. That's an archetypal thing. It's rebirth, spring, renewal, rebirth, living out of death, death rising into new life. It's just wonderful." She referred to these archetypes as her "spiritual constants" which she can use often with clients "without actually sounding terribly spiritual." She spoke of the archetype of transformation or redemption as a great theme in the Catholic Church, Jesus' dying and rising. Although her Catholic faith and the Easter liturgy provided the basis for her experience of transformation, Cunningham said, "All mankind needs redemption. It's a human thing. It's a general universal thing."

She elaborated on her own experience of this process of redemption or transformation as beginning in her childhood and developing into her adulthood. She spoke of this experience as,

> feeling that rejuvenation and the chance to live after the darkness of sin, and coming into the light and feeling free and wonderful. Not that sin was such a heavy presence on my mind. There is that chance to be free of all that through Easter, through the sacrifice of Jesus. That was the center of my meditation, gratitude for that, the joyousness of that, the sadness of my own contribution to the darkness that caused that crucifixion, used both literally and generally. Crucifixion would stand for any suffering that is incurred through man's foible and weaknesses and sins. But, you have a chance to be free of all that. In Catholic doctrine Jesus buys you back through his sacrifice. It's wonderful. Easter is that moment of freedom. So, that was just unbelievably rich for me.

Cunningham spoke of her years dealing with spiritual suffering, the pain of "dark sadness," which led to a happier feeling spiritually. She described then going through a parallel process psychologically in her Jungian analysis in which she faced her "shadow side." She referred to this experience as "horrible agony," but also, the freedom of joining your dark side with your light side. It's like another redemption. That's what consciousness really is about, individuation. You're not burdened with it. The dark doesn't have to eat you up. That's who I am. It's okay. Accepting that. It was a parallel motion with . . . the spiritual thing.

She explained her view that clients go through a similar process of transformation in which they must meet their shadow side, sometimes masked by bravado, without allowing it to increase their sense of self-condemnation. She spoke of clients working through this process and eventually coming to a place of fuller self-knowledge and acceptance of themselves as good enough. Cunningham referred to this as "a path of consciousness where dark and light are joined. And they really know that's who they are and that's okay."

Reflecting on this path of consciousness for herself, she stated,

That path is gone. I suppose, like everything else in my life, the greatest moments of enlightenment in my life are past. I'm not having great moments of enlightenment on that right now. I kind of had it. I don't know where I am right now. I don't know what's ahead of me. I just plod along.

She expressed her belief that in spirituality one must be conscious of one's nature and where one "is falling morally flat or low." She stated that psychologically one must realize where one is repressing, not accepting, or not allowing oneself to be conscious of one's "dark side." She said,

You have to work to get that up into light and consciousness. You have to keep working on these things. In the one case you end up maybe a saint, and here you end up individuated. I don't know if the two are the same. It's a struggle. It's a long road, and you can't let up. And boy, does it take discipline. I don't know, I think that's what I'm lacking right now is discipline. Too many grandchildren.

In responding to the question of if she had ever experienced her spirituality as negatively impacting or inhibiting the effectiveness of her clinical work, Ms. Cunningham stated that at times when she was a little younger she was somewhat over-eager to see clients progress faster than they could. She noted that she thinks of this as part of her "spiritual eagerness." She explained her view that when a therapist is over-eager the client at times will try to rush to match what they perceive the therapist to want without actually doing the work. She said that she watches that she does not do this and feels that it is not as critical for her now as in a former time in her practice. Cunningham referred to this over-eagerness as "wanting everybody to see everything you see, from the way you see it. It's very immature."

She offered a clinical example of this from her work with a young woman. Cunningham said that this woman "looked like she had just everything. She did, but she was very undeveloped in everything." She explained that this client was involved with a lot of things spiritually. Cunningham reflected that in her countertransference she felt that perhaps she viewed this client as more capable than she actually was and therefore she "pushed her" at a pace that was inappropriate for the client. Cunningham commented that she believes it was partially more experience as a therapist that would have helped her to deal with this situation with more wisdom. She stated that she tries to be very careful to be as conscious as possible about what messages she sends to her clients. She spoke of consulting with other colleagues. Still, she said, "What slips by, I guess slips by. I am who I am."

In closing, Ms. Cunningham said that she thinks being a psychotherapist "is a really good life." She stated that although others may perceive therapists as having a lot of power, her view of the therapist includes more of an element of self-sacrifice, "a servant to the well-being of this client." She noted that being a therapist is hard work which carries with it a lot of responsibility, as well as joy in seeing people feel better and become happier. Referring to the image from the Book of Isaiah, Cunningham spoke of therapists as "Suffering Servants." She concluded, "We are the servant of the people, the healing, hopefully helping-to-be-healed, servant of the people."

Core Themes

The following core themes were identified from the interviews as common to all or most participants. Each core theme will be further discussed in Chapter Four.

1. Each participant pointed to a development of their spirituality which is reflected in their current practice. While each came from Christian families of origin, each participant spoke of the important expanding influence of other spiritual traditions on their development.

2. In varying ways, each participant stated that their choice to become a psychotherapist was significantly influenced by and integral to their spirituality.

3. In varying ways, each participant spoke of their spirituality as significantly influencing their view of the human person as spiritual by nature and that psychological and spiritual development are in continuity or integral to one another. All participants viewed their work as psychotherapists as potentially promoting the spiritual healing and development of their clients.

4. In varying ways, all participants spoke of the importance to them of respecting the freedom and pace of their clients, particularly in regard to the integration of spirituality into the psychotherapy process.

5. All participants spoke of the importance of prayer or meditation for their own spiritual lives and for the enhancement of their clinical work.

6. Four of the five participants spoke of their spirituality as serving their capacity for compassion or to intuitively attune to their clients in therapy.

CHAPTER FOUR

DISCUSSION

Each core theme stated at the end of Chapter Three broadly reflects an idea which was found to be common to all or most participants. In most instances, the particular ways in which participants expressed the core themes were varied. This chapter will include an elaboration of the core themes with examples of how each theme was expressed by some or all participants, as well as a discussion of some of the significant variability found among participants. In addition, limitations of the study and suggestions for further research will be addressed.

Core Themes

Development

In the process of describing the nature of their spirituality in their lives currently, each participant pointed to an on-going developmental path for themselves, as opposed to a more static notion of their spiritual lives. Two common factors emerged as significant influences on the spiritual development of each participant. In the first case, each participant spoke in some way of how their own personal suffering or struggles had prompted the growth of their spiritual lives. For example, Torrano spoke of her own experience with depression as preparation for understanding others' spiritual and psychological suffering and eventually giving rise to a deepened sense of joy and intimacy currently in her relationship with God. Shaia spoke of his ongoing struggle to more fully integrate his sexuality as a man with his spiritual tradition. He spoke of this evolution as also reflected in his developing capacity to work with his male clients in regard to these issues.

The second significant factor influencing the spiritual development of all participants in various ways was each participant's encounters with spiritual traditions other than their own original Christian tradition. For example, Hutton spoke of his exploration of Eastern traditions as assisting him in understanding his own powerful spiritual experiences and his involvement with Native American spirituality as shaping his current "connection with the earth." Bragdon pointed to her in-depth exposure to Buddhism and Native American spirituality as a young adult as pivotal to the expansion of the rather limited spirituality of her family of origin. Torrano, Shaia, and Cunningham each also spoke of the growth-promoting influence of Buddhism, Hinduism, and/or Native American spirituality on their lives. In various ways, each of these three participants also spoke of the continued importance of their Catholic tradition on their present spiritual lives.

Professional Motivation

In considering the relationship between their spirituality and their choice of a profession as a psychotherapist, in various ways each participant spoke of an intimate connection. For example, both Hutton and Bragdon referred to the Buddhist concept of the way of the *bodhisattva*, compassionate devotion to assisting others who are suffering, as a central way in which they understood their original commitment to the work of psychotherapy. Torrano referred to her becoming a psychotherapist as a vocation or a call from God, a joyous feeling, and a gift which she could use to assist others to develop spiritually. Shaia spoke of his work as a psychotherapist as "discerning spirits in a very sacred space," in continuity with his many years of work in church ministry. He stated that the work of psychotherapy allows him to "follow the psyche or the soul without categories and restrictions" which he encountered with the institutional church.

View of the Person and the Aim of Psychotherapy

Fundamental to the impact of the participants' spirituality on their practice is their view of the human person and hence their view of the aim of their work as psychotherapists. In various ways, either explicitly or implicitly, all participants held a view of the human person, and therefore of their clients, as spiritual by nature. Hutton spoke of recognizing "a greater force is working" in therapy through him and everyone. Torrano referred to her heightening awareness of "the spiritual dimension" of her clients, while Cunningham said she finds "the underpinnings" of spirituality and transformation are present in the various clinical issues of her clients. Bragdon articulated this view as her appreciation not just for the highest human potential of her clients, but "first and foremost" her enjoyment and appreciation communicated in her presence of "the magnificence right here, right now" in the people with whom she works.

In addition to holding a fundamentally spiritual view of their clients, as I expected previous to the interviews, all participants in various ways also referred to their work as psychotherapists as potentially facilitating the spiritual healing and development of their clients. Although not necessarily stated explicitly to their clients, all participants viewed their work of facilitating psychological healing and development as integral to facilitating spiritual healing and growth. For example, Hutton referred to psychotherapy as a bridge that can help people become "reconnected to spiritual nature." Torrano expressed this in defining psychotherapy as "a means of touching and freeing the self God created one to be." Internally holding the view of his office as a chapel, Shaia spoke of his hope for his work as a psychotherapist to enable clients "to have a deep Self or soul experience which creates a new order or a new meaning in their life." Bragdon stated that she views her work as a psychotherapist as assisting others in their spiritual development, validating and helping clients make sense of their spiritual experience as it relates to their current life issues. Cunningham referred to the therapeutic work of the raising of one's consciousness as "a spiritual calling" and akin to "a moral imperative."

Respect for Clients' Freedom

While the majority of participants alluded to the fact that many of their clients come to them because of their reputation for spiritual integration in their clinical work, all participants in some way spoke of the importance to them of respecting the freedom of their clients, particularly in regard to their spirituality. For example, Hutton and Cunningham stressed being careful not to impose their own spirituality and religious views on to clients, following the lead of the client before pursuing spiritual issues. Shaia referred to his reverencing of clients by respecting their freedom and following their lead, viewing himself as a companion rather than as "the wisdom person" who knows more than the client what they need to do.

Prayer and Meditation

In varying ways all participants discussed the importance of prayer or meditation for their own spiritual lives and for the enhancement of their clinical work. For example, Hutton spoke of his daily practice of meditation as serving his capacity to be more present with his clients. While none of the participants spoke of praying with their clients, Torrano stated that when working with a suicidal or very difficult client she would often pray "to the God within that person" to spark the insight that would help the client through the impasse. She also stated that when she knew that a certain client prayed, at times she would ask the client about their experience of prayer regarding a particular issue. Hutton stated he would explore the issue of meditation with clients when they initiated the topic, Bragdon reported that she frequently helps clients find a spiritual practice to help them quiet their minds, and Cunningham claimed she sometimes suggests meditation or yoga to clients.

Compassion, Attunement, and Presence

Four of the five participants spoke of their spirituality as serving their capacity for compassion, to intuitively attune, and/or to be present with their clients. Hutton expressed this in terms of his own practices of meditation and guided visualization as sharpening his clinical intuition and attunement to his clients. Torrano described her capacity to closely attune emotionally and accurately intervene with clients as a spiritual resource to facilitate healing which goes beyond her mind, what she knows, and her particular personality style. She claimed her belief that this capacity is available to everyone and needs to be consciously cultivated by therapists. Besides heightening her intuition, Bragdon also described her spirituality in terms of deliberate attunement with "the deepest sacred nature in human beings and everything." Similar to Cunningham, Bragdon also spoke of her compassion toward clients as therapeutically inviting the same stance in clients toward themselves. Bragdon noted her belief that, generally speaking, compassion is the most important capacity for therapists to develop.

Significant Variability

Predominant Conceptualizations

While the core themes were found to be common to all or most participants, each participant differed, to varying degrees, in the overall predominant conceptualization or metaphor they used to express their spirituality and its impact on their practice. The diversity of predominant conceptualizations which were found across all cases also point to some differences in what participants emphasized about their spirituality and their practice. As expected before the interviews were conducted, the way in which each participant expressed their own current spirituality was found to be thematically similar to the predominant way in which they expressed it as informing their clinical practice. The following are the predominant ways in which each participant was found to have expressed their own spirituality and its impact on their work.

Hutton's spirituality was primarily described as shamanic, emphasizing a connection to nature, and the universality of religions. He emphasized his attempt to allow the working of a greater wisdom, healing force, or God, to be a part of his daily life. Hutton understood himself as allowing this healing energy to move in his "fairly traditional" psychotherapy practice through his own practice of meditation and prayer. He also saw this as occurring through his openness to exploring spirituality or any other material his clients may initiate.

Torrano's spirituality was primarily described as an intimate, personal relationship with God, with an emphasis on mystical religious experience. She primarily viewed psychotherapy as the work which assists in freeing a person to be who they truly are as created by God and thereby to allow for greater honesty and awareness in one's relationship with God. She understood her own spirituality as providing her with a growing awareness of and attention to the spiritual dimension of her clients and their healing processes.

Shaia's spirituality and his work with clients was primarily expressed using the interchangeable images of walking the labyrinth and an initiatory rite toward or away from an experience of Self, soul, or grace. Primarily informed by Jungian theory, he focused on his own understanding and experience with the movements of initiation (as spiritual development) as allowing him to accompany his clients through their own movements of healing and growth. Shaia emphasized his work with clients in sandplay as ritual space which facilitates their having an experience of the deep Self or soul.

Bragdon expressed her spirituality and her view of her work in psychotherapy as the expansion and freeing of consciousness that allows for access to bliss and a greater sense of deep connectedness with the sacred nature of "all that is." She emphasized the importance for her in psychotherapy of identifying with her own compassionate realm of consciousness and appreciating the magnificence of each client as ways to assist clients in becoming more compassionate toward themselves and better able to connect with their own spiritual nature.

Cunningham predominantly spoke of her spirituality and it's underpinnings in her psychotherapeutic work by using the Jungian concept of individuation and the Christian notion of redemption as an ongoing process of raising one's consciousness and transformation through the integration of one's shadow. This was expressed as a way to access the transcendent or the spiritual self.

While each participant emphasized different concepts or images with which to mediate their experience of their spirituality, it seems that overall the experience of the underlying process and reality to which each participant's conceptualization points is more similar than dissimilar. In varying ways all participants described their spiritual lives in terms of a process of seeking fuller access to divine, transcendent, or sacred experience. For example, Torrano referred to this experience as a personal relationship with God, Shaia used the language of an experience of Self, soul, or grace, and Bragdon spoke of it as connectedness with the sacred nature of "all that is." In varying ways all participants described this process, at least in part, as what they are trying to facilitate with their psychotherapy clients. For example, while Hutton referred to psychotherapy as a bridge that can assist people to become "reconnected to spiritual nature," Shaia spoke of his "hope and prayer" for his clients that through a process of reconciliation leading to an "interior communion" that they can "touch an experience of grace."

Other Important Themes

Other important specific themes or issues emerged from the set of five cases studied which were particular to only one or two participants. Some of these themes will be addressed here.

Hutton and Torrano in particular spoke about their belief in the significance of the impact of their own unconscious life on their clients. Hutton discussed this in the context of seeing the danger of unknowingly imposing his own spiritual interests on to his clients. Torrano referred to this dynamic more as a positive resource she offers, that as her own spirituality became more expansive and free, she has noticed that her clients became more free in sharing their spiritual experiences with her in therapy.

Hutton and Bragdon were the only participants who discussed cultivating a connection with nature as a primary focus for their spiritual lives. While Hutton stated he did not initiate conversations with clients about nature, Bragdon said she does encourage some clients to develop more of a healing relationship to the earth or to animals.

Cunningham was the only participant who explicitly spoke of her spirituality as significantly affecting her strong sense of professional ethics and integrity. She primarily expressed this in terms of her carefulness in watching her professional boundaries with her clients. However, all participants' concern to respect the freedom of their clients without imposing their own views or pace certainly also can be understood as their spirituality affecting their professional ethics. Cunningham and Hutton were the only participants who directly related their spirituality to the economic dimension of their practice. Cunningham spoke of her years of working for little or no pay in community mental health as, at least in part, a service out of love from her soul. Hutton noted his struggle to reconcile his spiritual value of assisting those in need with the collection of full fees from clients with limited financial resources.

Bragdon was unique among participants in her significant discussion of her capacity to address altered states of consciousness, near-death experiences, and past life experiences with her clients who have had these experiences.

Similar to my expectation for participants before the interviews were conducted, Torrano and Cunningham addressed their spirituality as providing meaning and trust in the face of psychological suffering. For example, Torrano spoke of the "rationale" of deep depression and psychological suffering sometimes offering the opportunity for greater appreciation for God's presence and activity. Cunningham expressed this as a faith in the arduous process of psychological individuation as parallel to spiritual redemption in which the pain of confronting and integrating one's sin or shadow side eventually bears greater freedom and joy. In both of these cases, the spirituality of the therapist serves to strengthen their sense of meaning, trust, and hope in the difficult therapeutic process.

Limitations of this Study

The present study was limited by the small number of participants. In as much as a larger sample pool would have allowed for a broader and more generalizable view of how various spiritually mature psychotherapists integrate their spirituality in their practice, the primary intention of this study was to provide an in-depth view of a small number of cases. Using an in-depth interview case studies methodology with a small number of participants allowed me to bring into relief the spirituality of psychotherapists with the anecdotes and particular language of participants themselves. This method seemed particularly fitting for the exploration and description of the rather subtle, multi-dimensional, and intuitive nature of spiritual experience. It also allowed for the reader to consider each participant more as a whole, in the context of each one's particular professional and spiritual background.

This study was also limited in scope and generalizability by the significant religious and cultural similarities of the participants. All participants stated that they were raised in predominantly Christian families of origin. Three of the five participants were raised within, and, in varying ways, were still significantly influenced by the Catholic tradition. Additionally, all five participants were Caucasian and raised within the United States. While the focus of this study was the living, operative experience of each participant's current spirituality broadly understood, certainly cultural and religious heritage are significant influences on how spirituality is experienced and expressed.

Suggestions for Further Research

Future research might examine the significance of the interaction between the particular religious or spiritual orientation of the psychotherapist and a different or similar orientation in their clients. In addition, it would be interesting to more closely study the resistance of some mental health professionals to spirituality and religion. The impact of the spirituality or religion of the client on their experience of their own healing and development in psychotherapy would also be a useful avenue of additional clinical research. Research which would support the development of greater systematic training in the integration of psychotherapy and spirituality and religion would be useful to facilitate a more holistic approach in psychotherapists' work with clients. Additional research is needed in general, particularly in this era of "managed care," to demonstrate further the benefits, including cost effectiveness, of healthcare services which provide for substantial attention to and care for the spiritual needs of patients. It is important to recall that the patient or client does not necessarily have to present as religiously oriented or concerned about their spiritual life or development for this type of integrated approach to be helpful. If such an orientation facilitates compassion for the patient or client as well as faith and hope in the healing process, all stand to benefit.

CHAPTER FIVE

CONCLUSIONS:
PSYCHOTHERAPY AS HOLY GROUND

One of the expectations with which I began this study was that participants, all of whom were identified as spiritually mature, would express a confidence in their capacity to address spiritual and religious issues raised by their clients. This expectation was supported by the research of Shafranske and Maloney (1990), as well as the view of Vaughan (1993) in her explanation of the practice of transpersonal psychotherapy. In various ways this expectation was confirmed by all participants. This study's participants, all of whom practice some form of a spiritually integrated approach to psychotherapy, all referred to their spirituality in some way as impacting the content of what was or could be competently addressed with their clients. For example, regarding one of her client's "quasi-tangible" experiences of God in prayer, Torrano stated, "The fact that I've experienced it, I can validate it." Similarly, Bragdon explained that she saw herself as assisting clients to recognize, validate, and to cognitively make sense of their spiritual experiences as they may relate to their other current life issues.

However, besides their competence to address the spiritual and religious topics raised by their clients, it was particularly interesting to find how participants emphasized their spirituality as impacting the way they practiced the process of psychotherapy itself. This was evidenced by several of the core themes. For example, the importance of respecting client's freedom, or therapists meditating in order to be more present to clients or praying to the God within the client, as well as compassion and intuitive attunement were issues addressed by all or most participants. These common core themes address more *how* the process of therapy is conducted rather than the content of *what* is discussed in psychotherapy.

In particular, Shaia conveyed an understanding of his spirituality and it's impact on his practice which appeared quite thoroughly integrated into the process of psychotherapy, with little or no emphasis on necessarily explicitly addressing clients' particular "religious" or "spiritual" issues as such. Though perhaps seen most clearly in the case of Shaia, it appears that because of the encompassing nature of each one's spirituality, all of the study's participants saw little, if any, separation between the spiritual dimension and any other dimension of human experience, particularly the psychological dimension. The experience of the process of psychotherapy itself is understood as a possible way to touch an experience of God or the spiritual dimension, rather than simply a place where such experiences can be talked about. What emerged from the data of the interviews was an experience and an understanding of the psychotherapists studied of the practice of psychotherapy itself as an inherently spiritual process. Although held by the psychotherapist, this perspective was not necessarily spoken or discussed explicitly with clients.

This understanding of psychotherapy is supported by the previously cited work of Byran Wittine (1993) who asserts that it is the spiritual world view and emerging awareness of "the Self" of the therapist that distinguishes transpersonal psychotherapy from other orientations, not necessarily the techniques practiced or the presenting problems of clients. Spero (1990) also was noted as supporting the possibility of a fully integrated view of psychotherapy itself as an expression or vehicle of a religious process. Using the concepts of a Christian theological view (Benner, 1983), it can be said that God's grace is understood as being incarnated within the interpersonal process of psychotherapy itself, rather than only as an issue to be talked about in psychotherapy. To view spirituality or religion only as something that can be talked *about* in psychotherapy is to unfortunately treat spirituality reductionistically and to perpetuate a dualistic approach to psychology and spirituality or religion. It is to risk separating and diminishing spirituality as a fundamental human experience into the more distant and less vital realm of reflection upon that experience. Reflection upon and exploration of one's religious and spiritual experiences and issues certainly can be an important aspect of what is addressed in psychotherapy. However, as evidenced by these participants, the process of psychotherapy itself, by the way it is conducted, also can be cultivated as holy ground to allow for more immediate spiritual and religious experience, and therefore for fuller healing and growth.

Cultivating the Ground: Implications for Clinical Practice and Training

As supported by the literature and evidenced by the present study, an approach to psychotherapy which is spiritually integrated can be understood as involving three key dimensions for the practitioner:

1. a spiritually integrated theoretical view of the nature and development of the human person and of the process of psychotherapy,

2. knowledge about various spiritual and religious issues and traditions, and

3. the experiential development of the psychotherapist's own spiritual life.

It is the cultivation of these three dimensions which allows practitioners to offer to their clients a spiritually integrated experience of psychotherapy which includes not only the content of what is addressed but also the process of the therapy itself. Each of these dimensions is important to address in the training of spiritually mature and integrated psychotherapists.

The first dimension provides the practitioner with a cognitive map for an overview of the terrain of human psycho-spiritual development and healing. Such a theoretical lens can help to ground and direct the practitioner in their efforts to accompany and at times guide the client on their journey of healing and development. Some of the available spiritually-integrated theoretical literature was reviewed in Chapter One. Additionally, within this dimension is included the competency to formulate a psychological assessment which integrates issues related to the religious and spiritual life of the client. Understanding is also necessary which allows the practitioner to appreciate something of what distinguishes healthy and pathological spirituality.

The second dimension, knowledge about various spiritual and religious traditions and issues, provides practitioners with the information necessary to better appreciate and respond to the varieties of religious and spiritual issues and experiences raised by their clients. In part, such understanding can be viewed as a part of the professional standard of cultural competence called for by contemporary mental health associations. This knowledge can also serve to enhance the spiritual development of the practitioner. The therapist's heightened awareness of their own religious and spiritual tradition, or lack thereof, as well as their biases, can reduce the likelihood of their countertransference becoming an obstacle to the client's free exploration and development of their own spirituality.

Thirdly and most importantly, the personal, experiential, spiritual development of the psychotherapist serves as the foundation for a spiritually integrated approach to psychotherapy. It is difficult or impossible to accompany or guide clients in territory which we as psychotherapists are unfamiliar. Beyond theory and technique, alongside clients, it is the person of the psychotherapist, specifically in the integrity and extent of their own psycho-spiritual development, that is the greatest resource in the therapeutic process. Continuing care must be given to the rejuvenation and growth of this resource in order to keep the practitioner vital and whole as a person and as a professional. Greater attention to the development of these three dimensions of spirituality in the training of mental health professionals will allow for further healing of the historic rift between psychotherapy and spirituality and significantly strengthen the effectiveness of our work as clinicians.

Appendix A

Screening Instrument

Instructions: After each of the four statements given below, please indicate the degree to which you personally agree or disagree with each statement as it relates to yourself by rating each statement with either a: 1 - strongly disagree, 2 - disagree, 3 - somewhat disagree, 4 - somewhat agree, 5 - agree, or 6 - strongly agree.

1. The development of my relationship with God/Other is a core value for my life.

2. My spiritual life relates in an important way to the major aspects of my daily life.

3. The development of my spiritual life has been a high priority for me for a long time.

4. I regularly participate in some form of prayer or meditation.

_____
Name

Appendix B

Interview Questions

Part I: Professional demographics and spiritual history (10-15 minutes)

1. What type of professional training have you received to practice psychotherapy? What type of academic degrees have you completed?

2. How long have you been licensed as a psychotherapist?

3. In what kind of setting do you now practice psychotherapy? What type of clients do you serve?

4. How would you describe your theoretical orientation as a psychotherapist?

5. Besides psychotherapy what other types of activities occupy your professional life?

6. If any, in what religious tradition were you raised as a child and/or adolescent?

7. What did your family of origin believe about spirituality? Was spirituality important? (Spirituality is here understood broadly as one's relationship with God)

8. What kinds of educational and spiritual development experiences have you had which have been important to the development of your spiritual life? For example: the academic study of religion or spirituality, professional training for spiritual/ministerial leadership, retreats, involvement with a particular church or religious

community, or participation in a spiritual direction/companionship relationship.

9.   If any, what is your current religious affiliation?

Part II: Current spirituality and its impact on the practice of psychotherapy.

1.   How would you describe the nature of spirituality in your life now? (5-10 minutes)

2.   If any, what impact did your spirituality have on your choice to become a psychotherapist? (5-10 minutes)

3.   How do you experience your spirituality as impacting the way you practice psychotherapy? (45-55 minutes)

     a.   How does your spirituality affect your view of who you are in your practice as a psychotherapist?

     b.   How does your spirituality affect your view of what you are doing in your practice as a psychotherapist?

     c.   How do you experience your spirituality as providing a resource for facilitating the psychological healing and growth of clients in your practice? Would you describe some clinical examples of this?

     d.   Have you ever experienced your spirituality as negatively impacting or inhibiting the effectiveness of your clinical work? If yes, how would you describe this experience? Would you describe some clinical examples of this?

4.   Is there anything further that you would like to say at this time? Please feel free to do so now.

Bibliography

Allport, G.W. (1950). *The individual and his religion.* New York: MacMillan.

American Psychiatric Association (1994). *Diagnostic and statistical manual of mental disorders (4th ed.).* Washington, D.C.: Author.

Benner, D.G. (1983). The incarnation as a metaphor for psychotherapy. *Journal of Psychology and Theology, 11,* 287-294.

Bergin, A.E. (1991). Values and religious issues in psychotherapy and mental health. 98th Annual Convention of the American Psychological Association Distinguished Professional Contributions Award Address (1990, Boston, MA). *American Psychologist, 46,* 394-403.

Bergin, A.E. & Jensen, J.P. (1990). Religiosity of psychotherapists: A national survey. *Psychotherapy, 33,* 3-7.

Bradford, D.T., & Spero, M.H. (Eds.). (1990). Psychotherapy and religion {Special issue}. *Psychotherapy, 27 (1).*

Burton, L.A. (Ed.). (1992). *Religion and the family: When God helps.* Binghamton: New York: Haworth Pastoral Press.

Calestro. (1972). Psychotherapy, faith-healing, and suggestion. *International Journal of Psychiatry, 90,* 83-113.

Ellis, A. (1980). Psychotherapy and atheistic values: A response to A.E. Bergin's "Psychotherapy and religious values." *Journal of Consulting and Clinical Psychology, 48,* 635-639.

Fowler, J.W. (1981). *Stages of faith.* San Francisco: Harper and Row.

111

Frankl, V.E. (1975). *The unconscious God.* New York: Simon and Schuster.

Freud, S. (1961). The future of an illusion. In J.Strachey (Ed. and Trans.), *The standard edition of the complete psychological works of Sigmund Freud* (Vol. 21, pp. 3-56). London: Hogarth Press. (Original work published 1927).

_____ (1973). The phenomenon of religion. In J.J. Heaney (Ed.), *Psyche and spirit.* New York: Paulist Press.

Friedman, M., Thoresen, C.E., Gill, J.J., Powell, L.H., Ulmer, D., Thompson, L., Price, V.A., Rabin, D.D., Breall, W.S., Dixon, T., Levy, R., & Bourge, E. (1984). Alteration of Type A behavior and reduction in cardiac recurrences in postmyocardial infarction patients. *American Heart Journal, 108,* 237-248.

Fromm, E. (1950). *Psychoanalysis and religion.* New Haven, Conn.: Yale University Press.

Gallup, G. (1985). Fifty years of Gallup surveys on religion. *The Gallup report.* Report No. 236.

Henning, L.H., & Tirrell, F.J. (1982). Counselor resistance to spiritual exploration. *Personnel and Guidance Journal, 10,* 92-95.

James, W. (1902). *The varieties of religious experience.* New York: Longman's Green.

Jung, C.G. (1933). *Modern man in search of a soul.* New York: Harcourt Brace Jovanovich, Publishers.

Kung, H. (1990). *Freud and the problem of God.* New Haven, CT: Yale University Press.

Lannert, J.L. (1991). Resistance and countertransference issues with spiritual and religious clients. *Journal of Humanistic Psychology, 31,* 68-76.

_____ (1991). Spiritual and religious values of training directors and their internship sites. Unpublished doctoral dissertation, University of Southern California, Los Angeles.

Lovinger, R.L. (1984). *Working with religious issues in psychotherapy.* New York: Jason Aronson.

Lukoff, D., Turner, R., & Lu, F. (1992). Transpersonal psychology research review: Psychoreligious dimensions of healing. *Journal of Transpersonal Psychology, 24,* 41-60.

_____ (1993). Transpersonal psychology research review: Psychospiritual dimensions of healing. *Journal of Transpersonal Psychology, 25,* 11-28.

Martin, J.E., & Carlson, C.R. (1988). Spiritual dimensions of health psychology. In W.R. Miller and J.E. Martin (Eds.), *Behavior therapy and religion: Integrating spiritual and behavioral approaches to change* (pp. 57-110). Newbury Park, CA: Sage Publications.

Maslow, A.H. (1964). *Religion, values, and peak-experiences.* Columbus: Ohio State University Press.

_____ (1970). *Motivation and personality* (2nd ed.). New York: Harper & Row. (First edition 1954)

May, G.G. (1982). *Will and spirit: A contemplative psychology.* San Francisco: Harper & Row.

_____ (1988). *Addiction and grace.* San Francisco: Harper & Row.

Miller, W.R., & Martin, J.E. (Eds.). (1988). *Behavior therapy and religion: Integrating spiritual and behavioral approaches to change.* Newbury Park, CA: Sage Publications.

Noam, G.G. & Wolf, M. (1993). Psychology and spirituality: Forging a new relationship. In M.L. Randour (Ed.), *Exploring sacred landscapes: Religious and spiritual experiences in psychotherapy.* New York: Columbia University Press.

Oden, J. (1967). *Contemporary theology and psychotherapy.* Philadelphia: Westminster.

Payne, I.R., Bergin, A.E., & Loftus, P.E. (1992). A review of attempts to integrate spiritual and standard psychotherapy techniques. *Journal of Psychotherapy Integration,* 171-192.

Peck, M.S. (1993). *Further along the road less traveled: The unending journey toward spiritual growth.* New York: Simon & Schuster.

Peterson, E.A. & Nelson, K. (1987). How to meet your clients' spiritual needs. *Journal of Psychosocial Nursing, 25,* 34-39.

Powell, L.H., Thoresen, C.E., Friedman, M., et al. (1986, March). Clinical techniques to alter the 'Type A' behavior pattern: Part 2 - Alteration of the the Type A attitudes and beliefs. Workshop presented before the Society of Behavioral Medicine, San Francisco, CA.

Propst, L.R. (1988). *Psychotherapy in a religious framework: Spirituality in the emotional healing process.* New York: Human Sciences Press.

Propst, L.R., Ostrom, R., Watkins, P., Dean, T., & Mashburn, D. (1992). Comparative efficacy of religious and non-religious cognitive-behavioral therapy for the treatment of clinical depression in religious individuals. *Journal of Consulting and Clinical Psychology, 60,* 94-103.

Ragan, C. & Maloney, H.N. (1976). The study of 'religiosity': its history and its future. *Journal of Psychology and Theology, 4,* 128-140.

Randour, M.L. (Ed.). (1993) *Exploring sacred landscapes: Religious and spiritual experiences in psychotherapy.* New York: Columbia University Press.

Rizzuto, A. (1993). In M.L. Randour (Ed.), *Exploring sacred landscapes: Religious and spiritual experiences in psychotherapy.* New York: Columbia University Press.

Shafranske, E.P. (Ed.). (1996) *Religion and the clinical practice of psychology.* Washington, D.C.: American Psychological Association.

Shafranske, E.P. & Gorsuch, R.L. (1984). Factors associated with the perception of spirituality in psychotherapy. *The Journal of Transpersonal Psychology, 16,* 231-241.

Shafranske, E.P. & Maloney, H.N. (1990). Clinical psychologists' religious and spiritual orientations and their practice of psychotherapy. *Psychotherapy, 27,* 72-78.

Spero, M.H. (1985). Theoretical and clinical aspects of transference as a religious phenomenon in psychotherapy. *Journal of Religion and Health, 24,* 8-25.

_____ (1990). Parallel dimensions of experience in psychoanalytic psychotherapy of the religious patient. *Psychotherapy, 27,* 53-71.

Sutich, A. J. (1969). Some considerations regarding transpersonal psychology. *Journal of Transpersonal Psychology, 1,* 11-20.

Thoresen, C. (1987, June). *Development and modification of Type A behavior patterns.* Paper presented at San Diego State University Summer Symposium, "Type A Coronary Prone Behavior Pattern: A Comprehensive Look," San Diego, CA.

Wittine, B. (1993). Assumptions of transpersonal psychotherapy. In R. Walsh & F. Vaughan (Eds.), *Paths beyond ego: The transpersonal vision.* Los Angeles, CA: Jeremy P. Tarcher, Inc.

Wulff, D.M. (1991). *Psychology of religion: Classic and contemporary views.* New York: John Wiley & Sons.

Vaughan, F. (1993). Healing and wholeness: Transpersonal psychotherapy. In R. Walsh & F. Vaughan (Eds.), *Paths beyond ego: The transpersonal vision*. Los Angeles, CA: Jeremy P. Tarcher, Inc.

Index

Adler, A., 4
Allport, G.W., 5, 6, 23, 24
altered states, 75, 98
American Psychological Association, xiii, xvi, 2, 8, 47
animal, 37, 72, 97
archetype, 12, 55, 57, 85, 86
Avatar, 67, 68

Benner, D. G., 12, 104
Bergin, A. E., xiv-xvi, 8, 9, 11, 13-15
bliss, 70, 71, 96
bodhisattva, 35, 71, 92
Buddha, 83
Buddhism, 6, 33, 35, 69-71, 80, 92
Burton, L. A., 10

Calestro, 1
Carlson, C. R., 10
case study, 3, 19, 98
Catholic, 41, 43, 45, 56-60, 63, 79-81, 86, 92, 99, 127
chastity, 44
Christ, 9, 12, 82

Christian, 1, 9, 12, 60, 89, 92, 96, 99, 104
Christianity, 1, 33
church, xiv, xv, 2, 5, 32, 34, 43, 45, 55-58, 60, 63, 68, 81, 86, 92, 109
clinical psychology, 8, 31, 55
cognitive-behavioral, 9, 10
collective unconscious, 4
communion, 25, 42, 59, 64, 97
community, 1, 20, 32, 43, 45, 56-59, 69, 109
compassion, 12, 32, 35, 52, 71-74, 83, 89, 92, 94-96, 100, 103
connectedness, 32, 35, 38, 70-72, 85, 93, 96, 97
consciousness, 12, 37, 38, 51, 52, 68, 72, 76, 85-87, 93, 96
contemplative spirituality, 9
countertransference, 14, 88, 106
cultural, 1, 2, 51, 58, 99, 106
culture, 1, 4, 57, 64
cure of souls, 1

Dass, R., 71
death, 75, 79, 84-86, 98

117

About the Author

John P. Sullivan is a native of San Jose, California. He received his bachelor's degree in psychology and theology from Loyola Marymount University in Los Angeles in 1983. After teaching high school and doing youth ministry in Belize, Central America, he earned a Master of Divinity degree in 1987 from Weston Jesuit School of Theology in Cambridge, Massachusetts. He has been certified by the National Association of Catholic Chaplains since 1988 and has worked as a hospital chaplain in California and Massachusetts. In 1997 he completed the Doctor of Psychology degree in clinical psychology from California School of Professional Psychology in Berkeley/Alameda. His clinical training has included work in Spanish and English with children, adolescents, and adults in community mental health centers. He completed advanced training in the integration of psychotherapy and spirituality at The Danielsen Institute at Boston University.